MOROCCO

Marrakech and the Sahara

a photo-book by Christian Cantelli Podestà

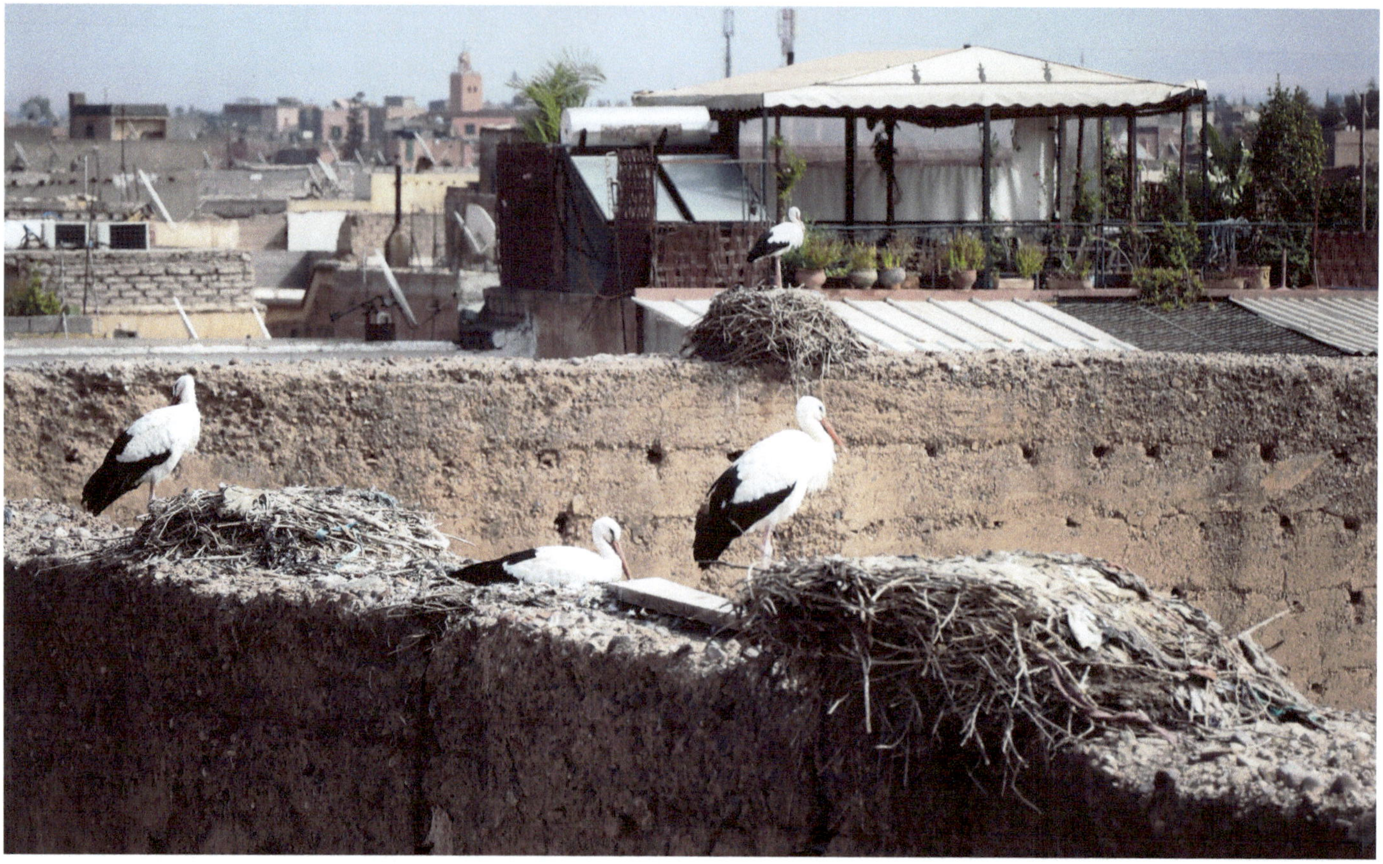

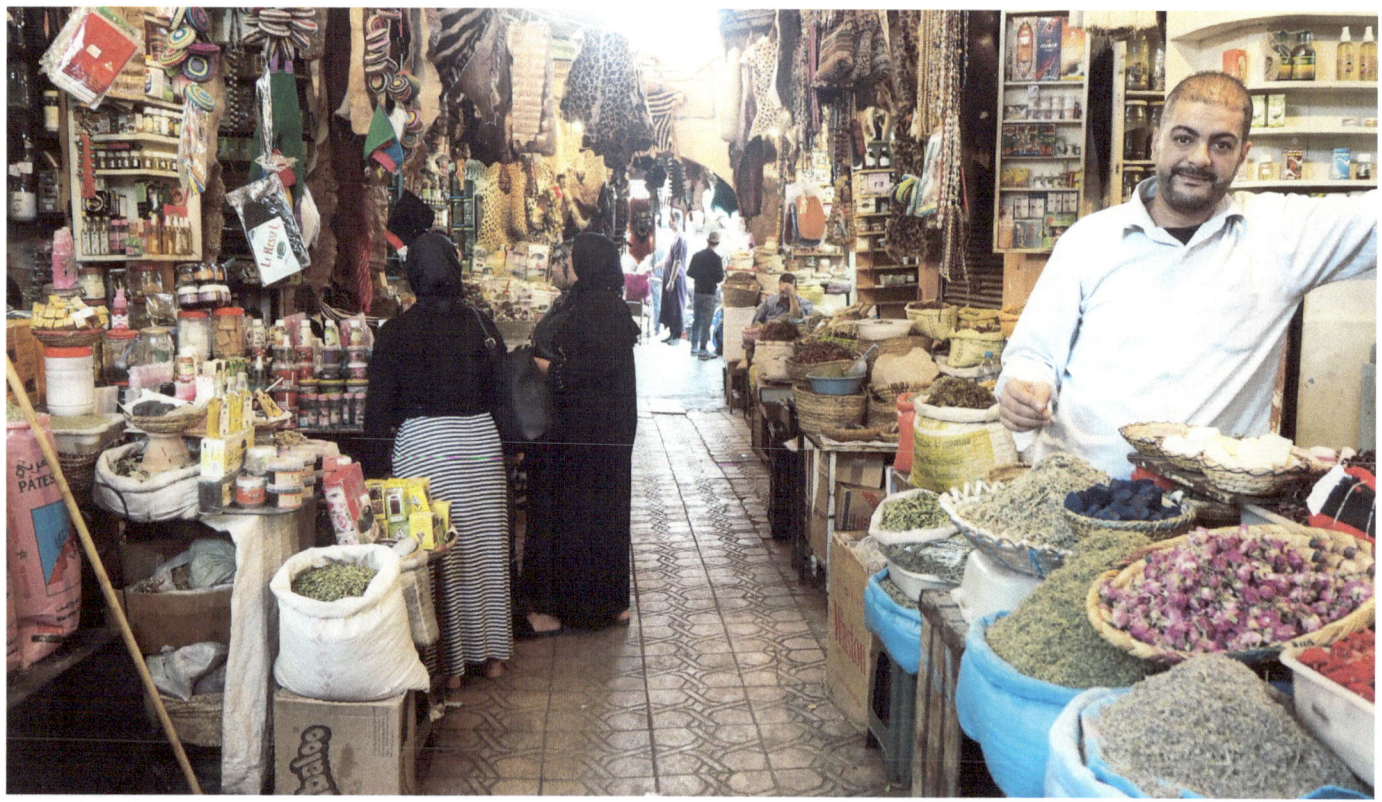

Marrakech is a major city of the Kingdom of Morocco. It is the fourth largest city in the country; Like many Moroccan cities, Marrakesh comprises an old fortified city packed with vendors and their stalls, the Medina.

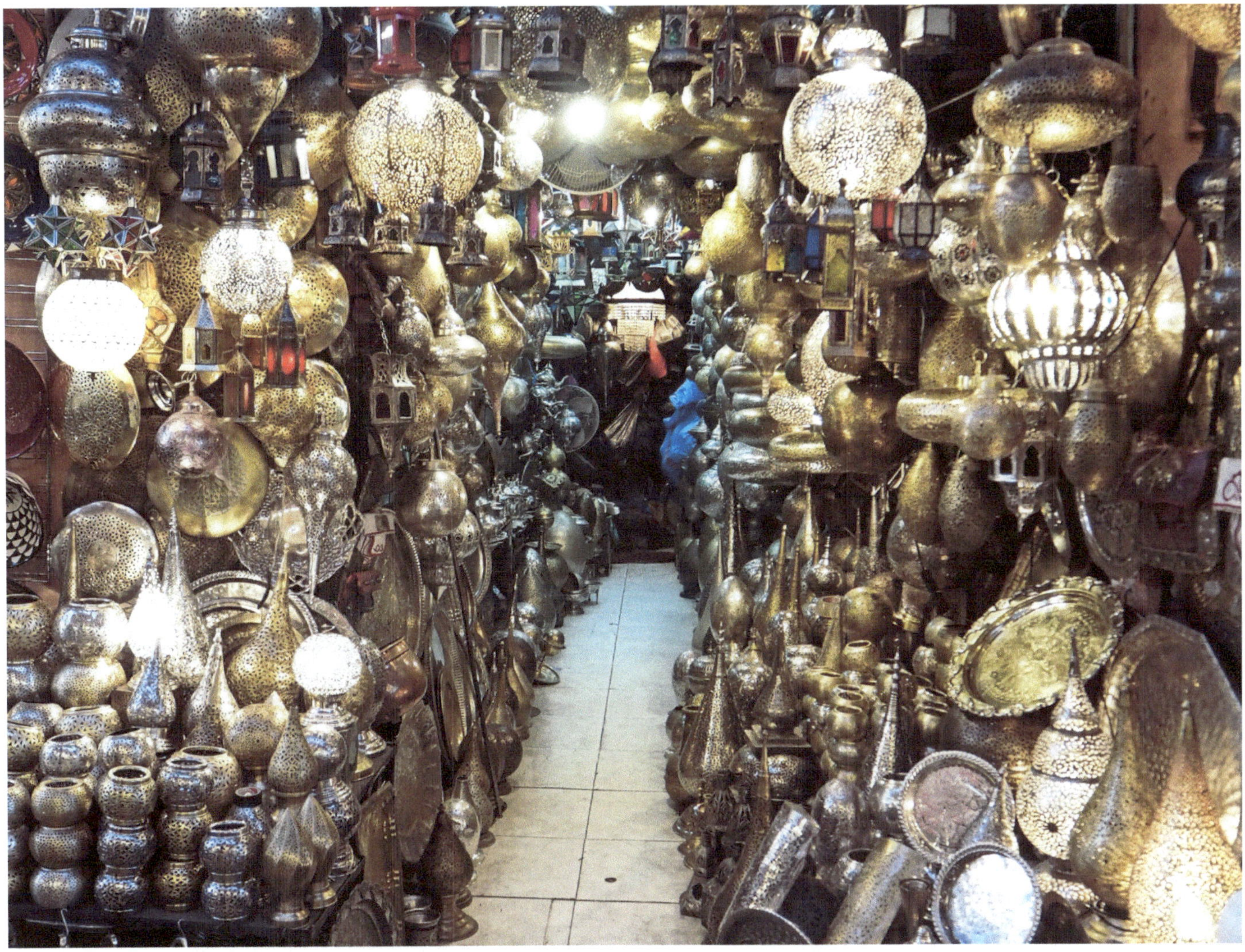

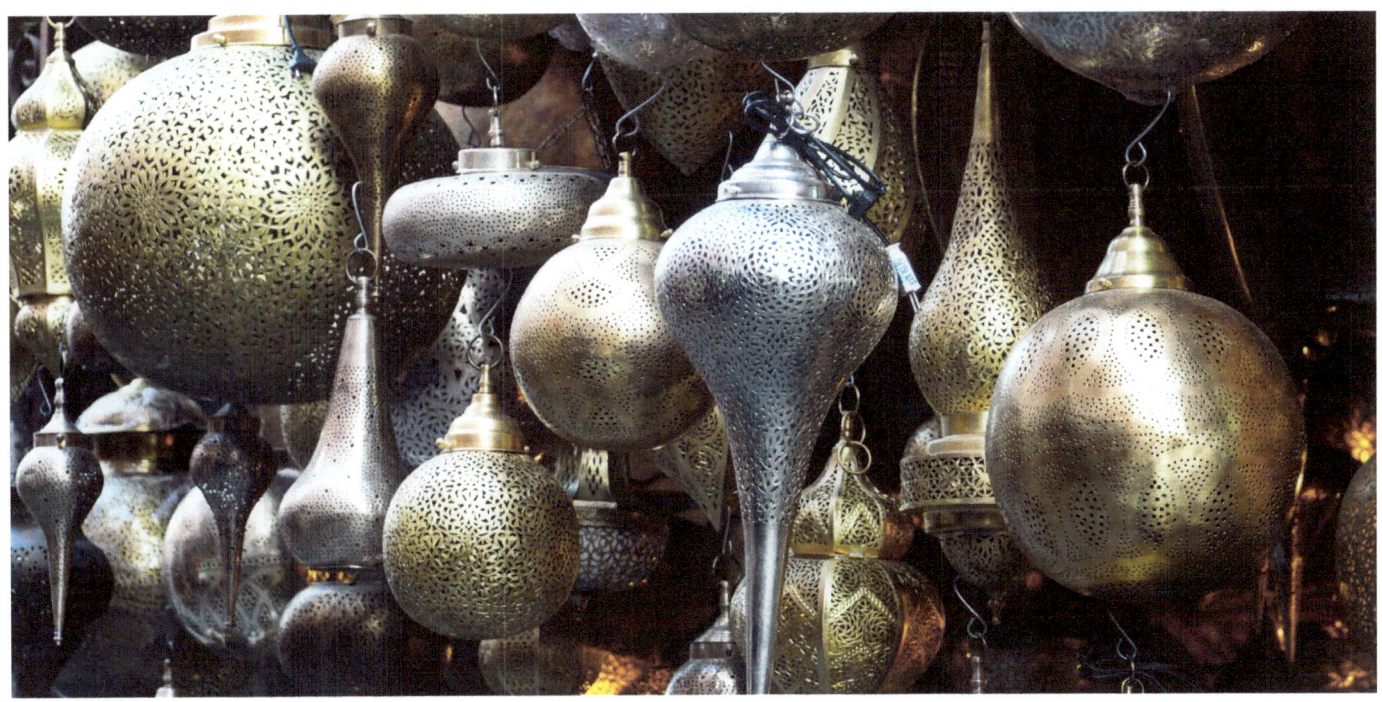

Every little shop inside the Medina is a magical hall of wonders.

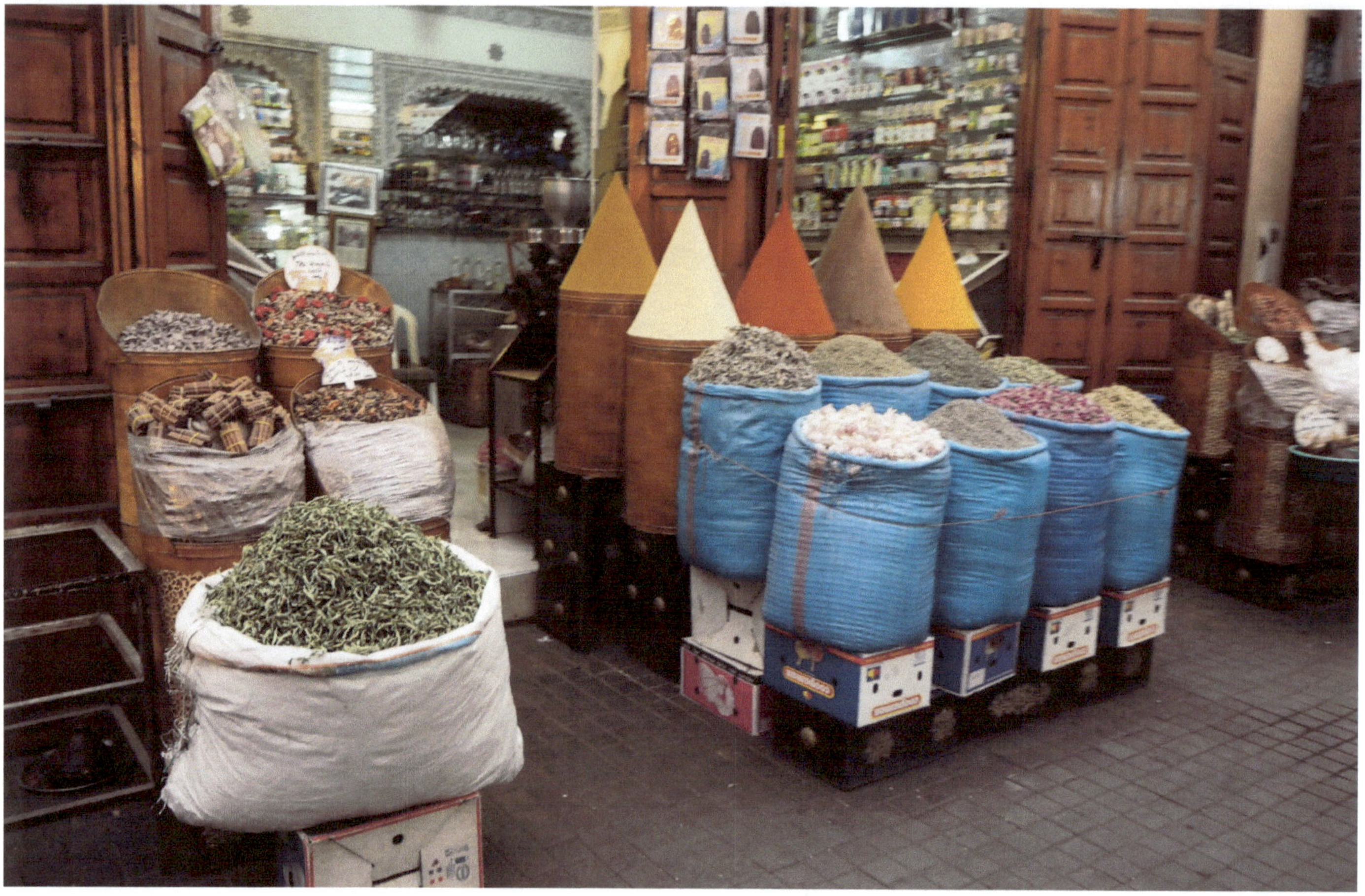

Moroccans take spices very seriously

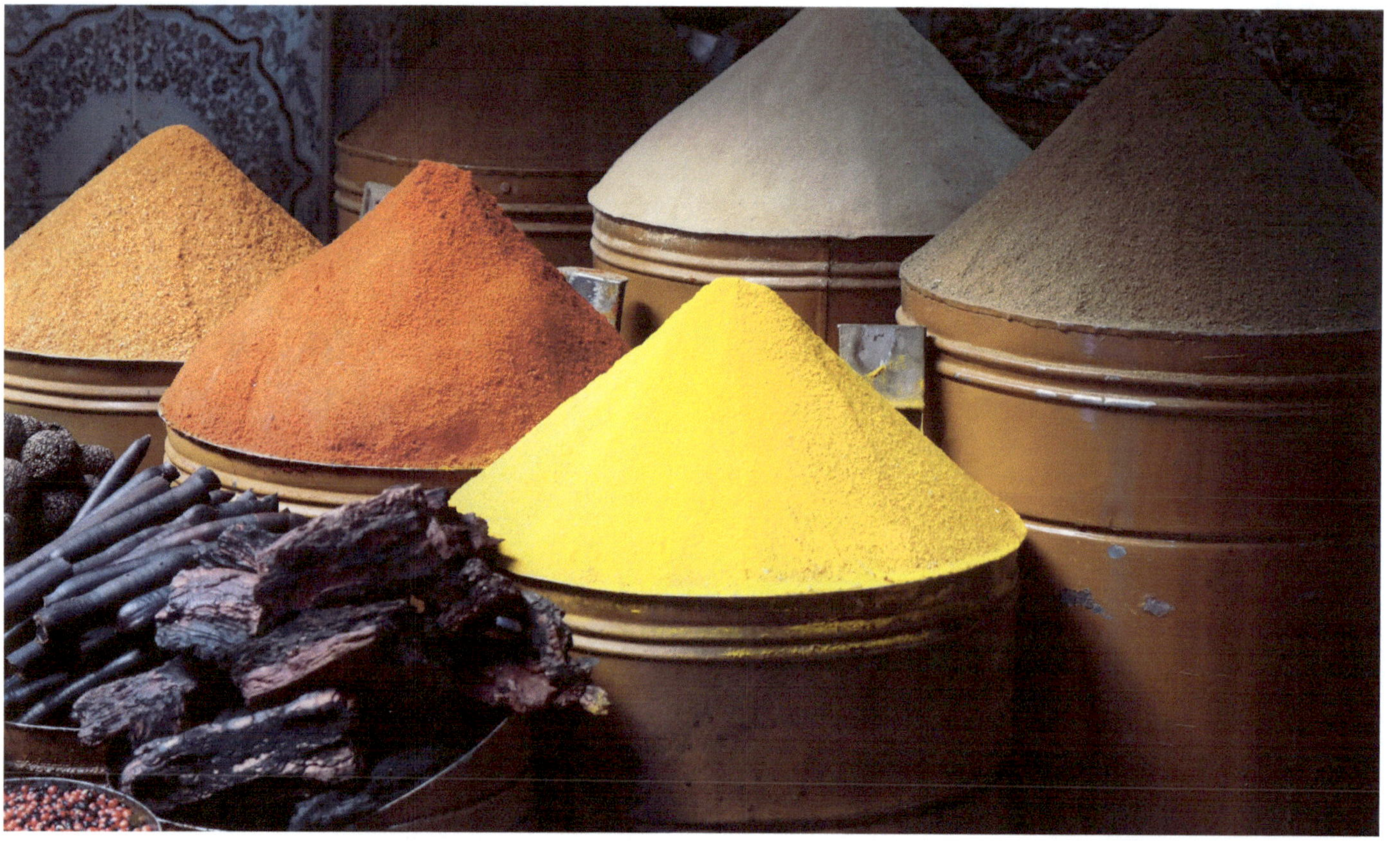

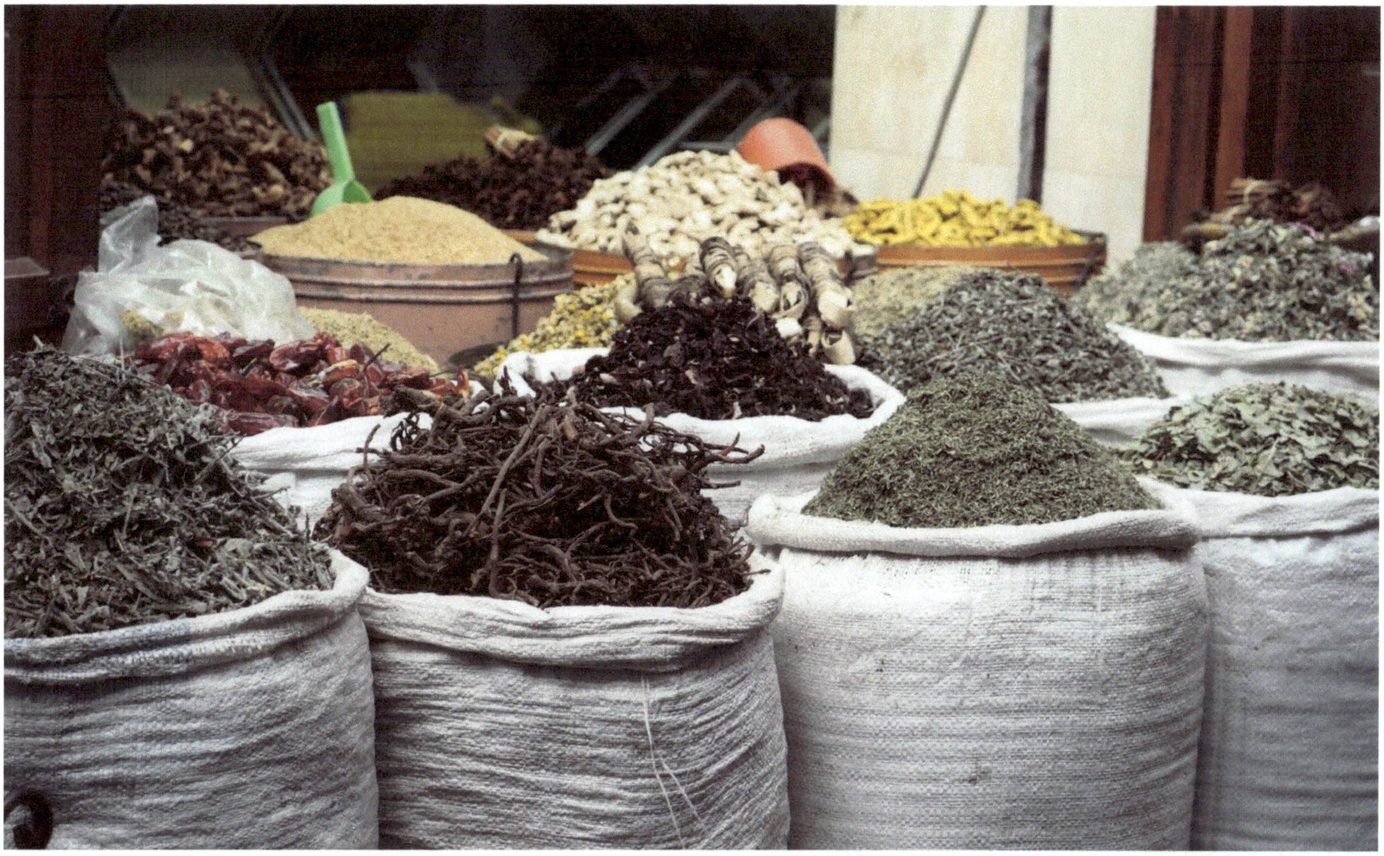

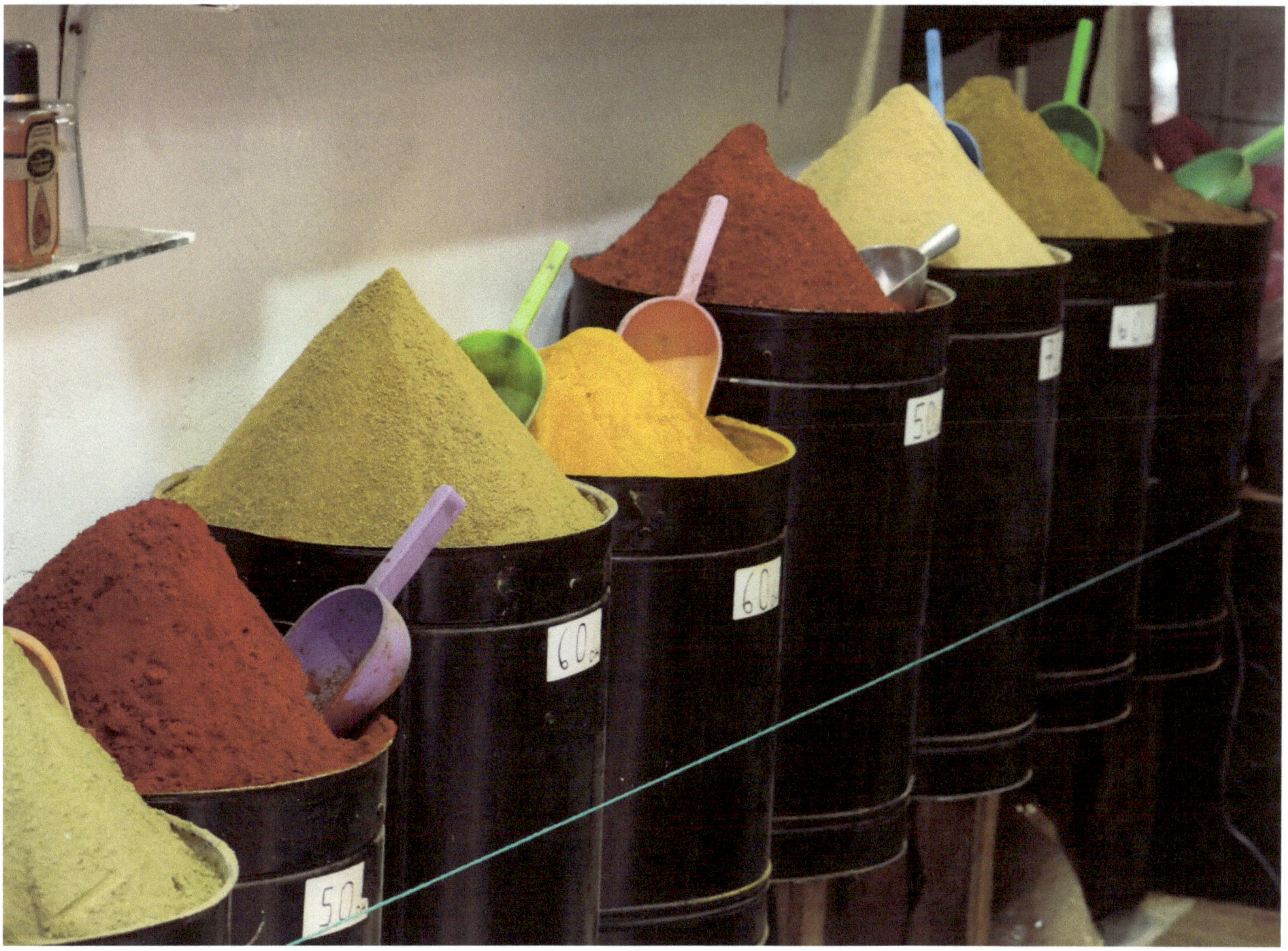

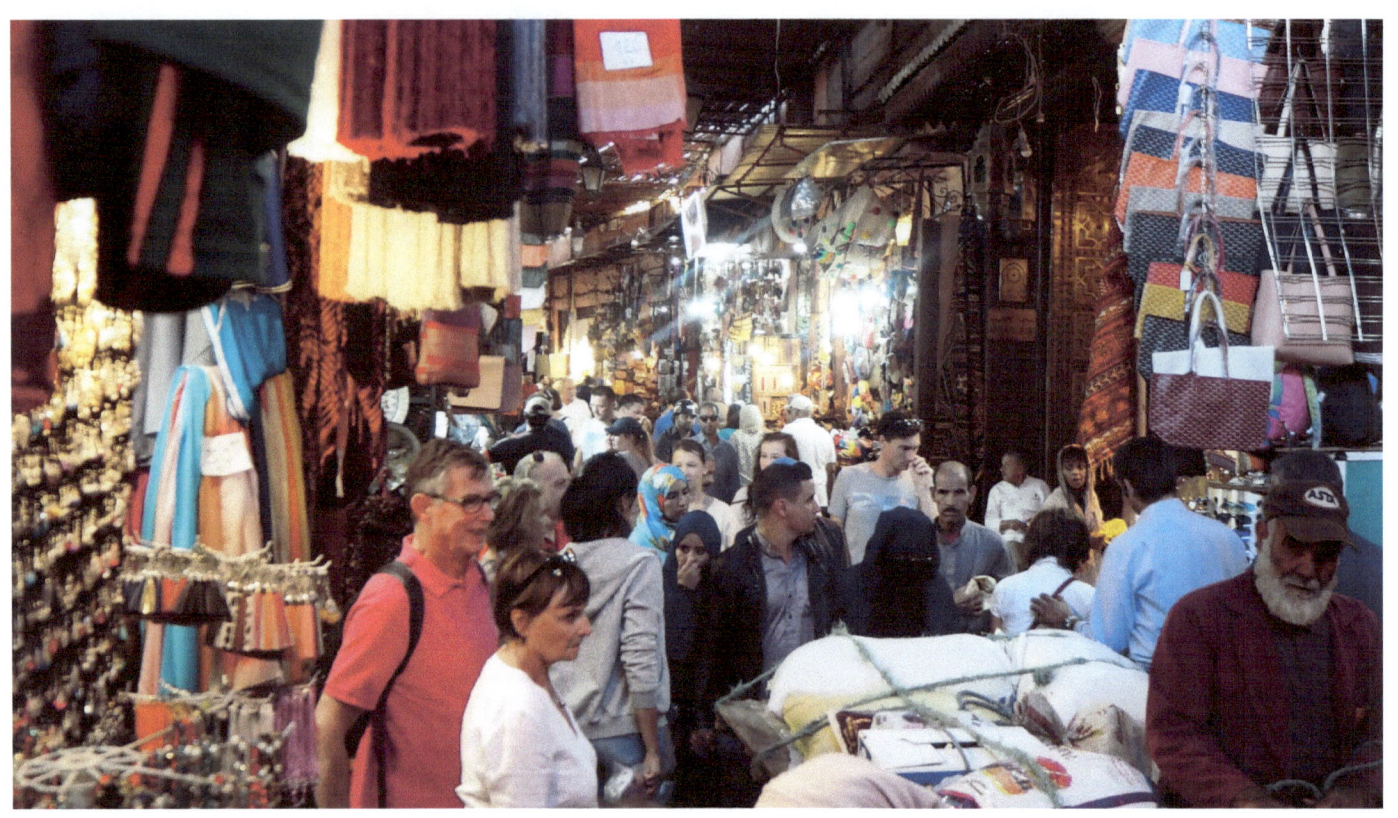

These chaotic alleys are always full of locals and tourists at all hours of the day

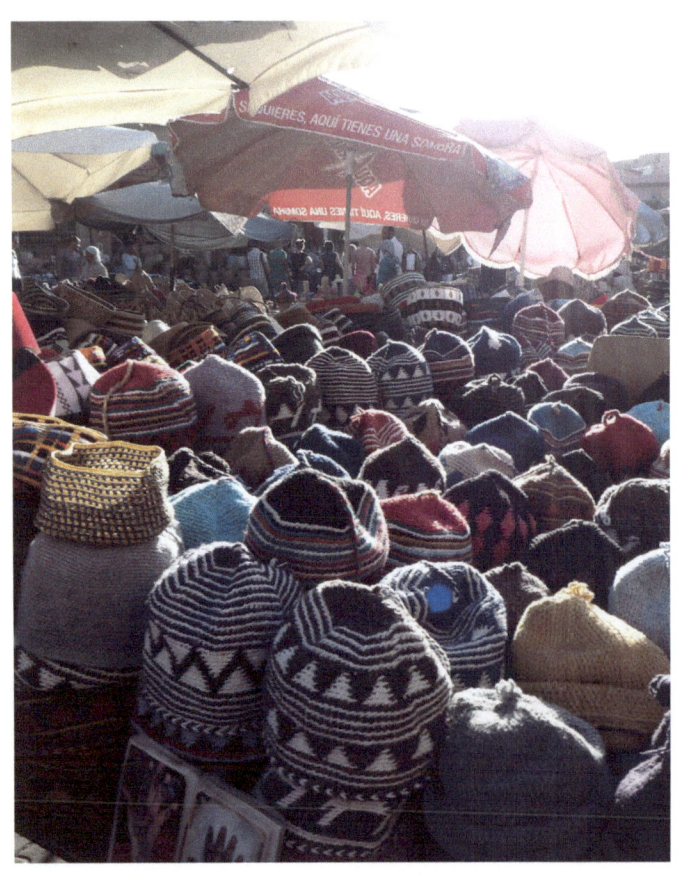

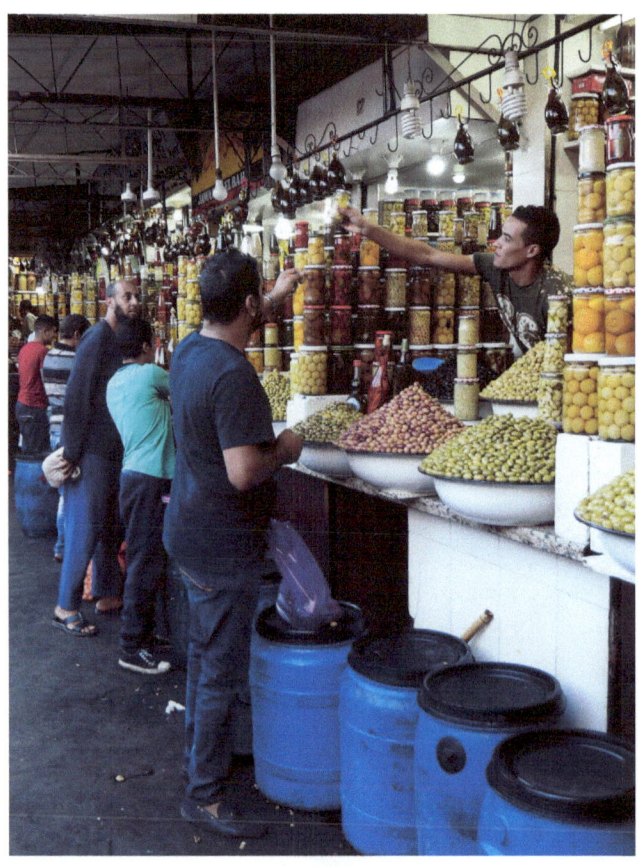

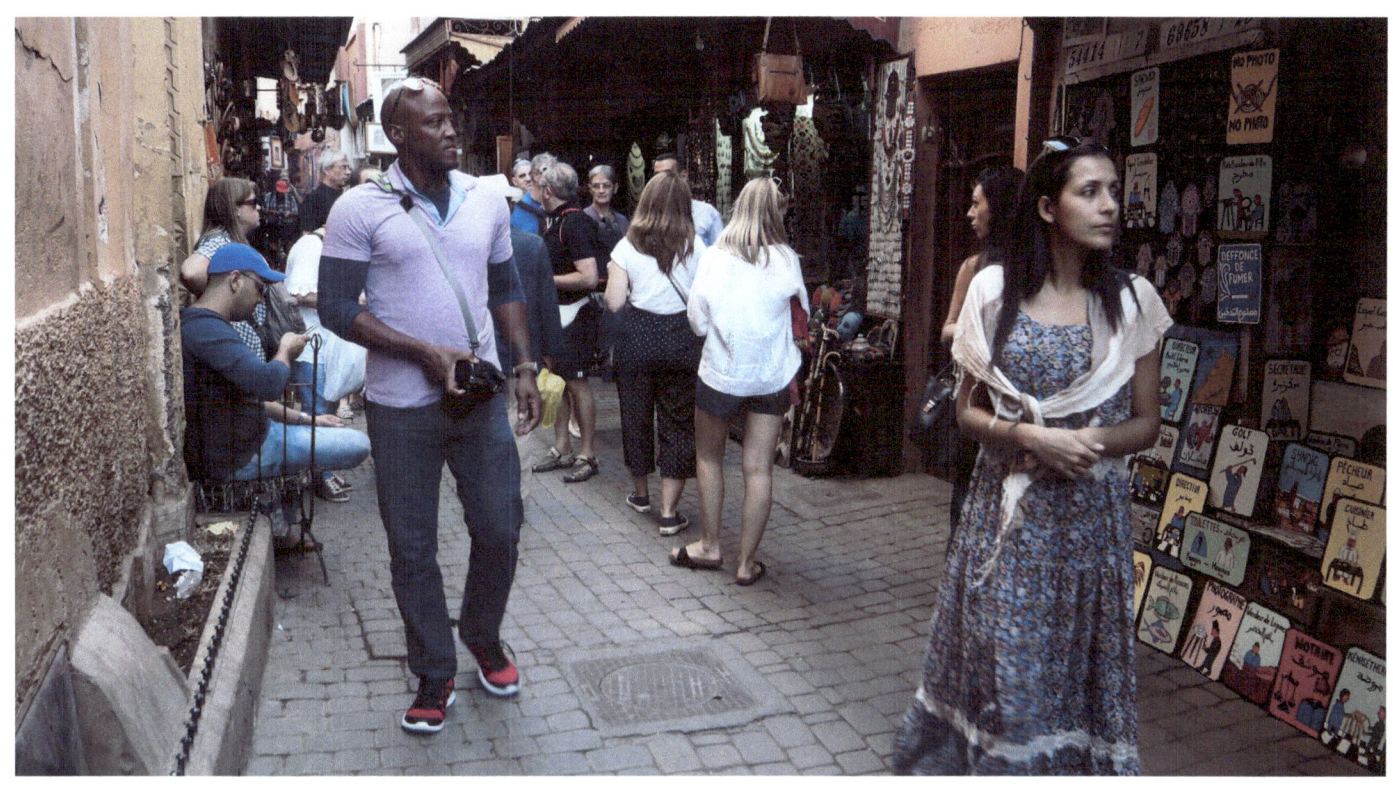

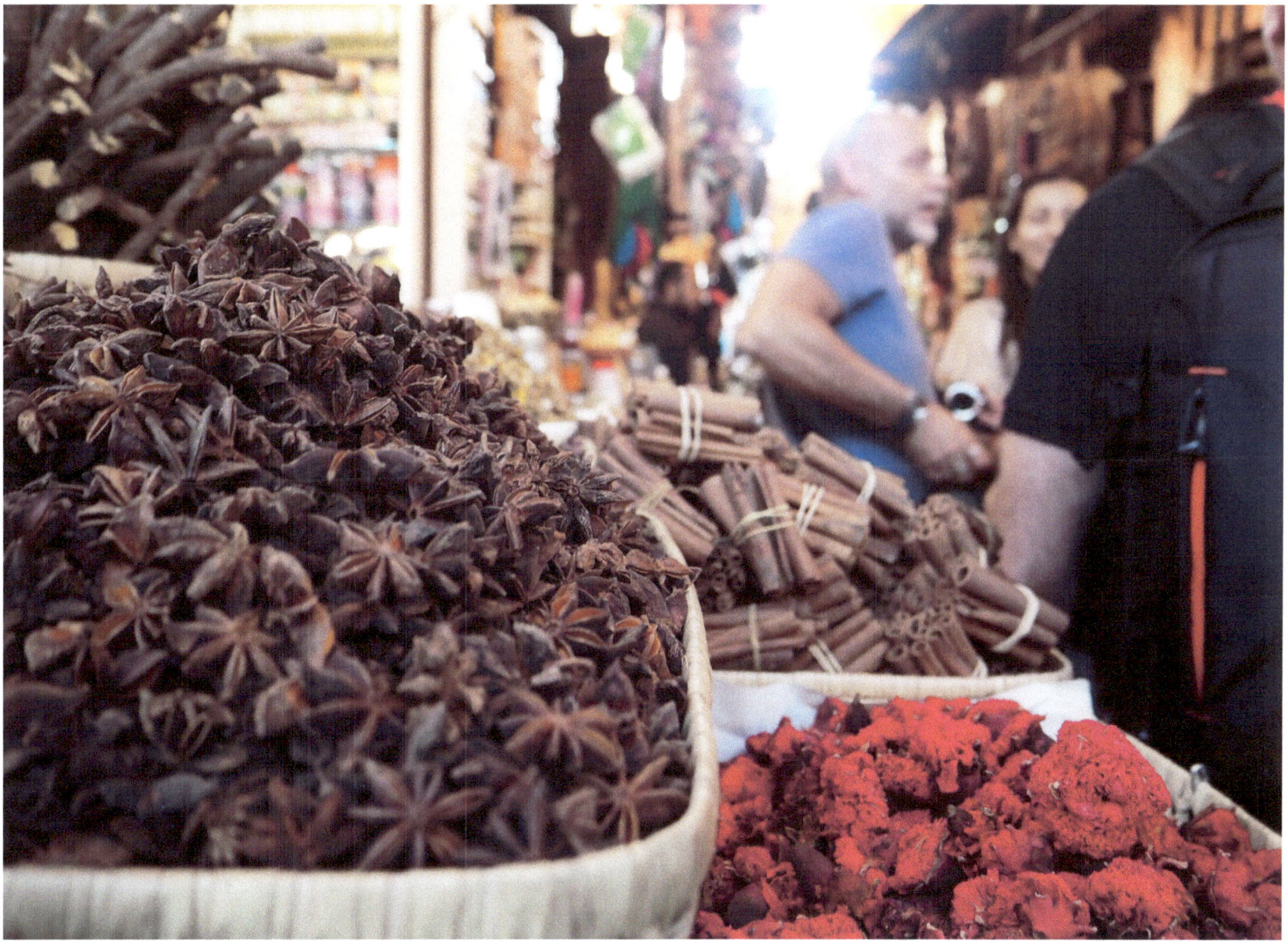

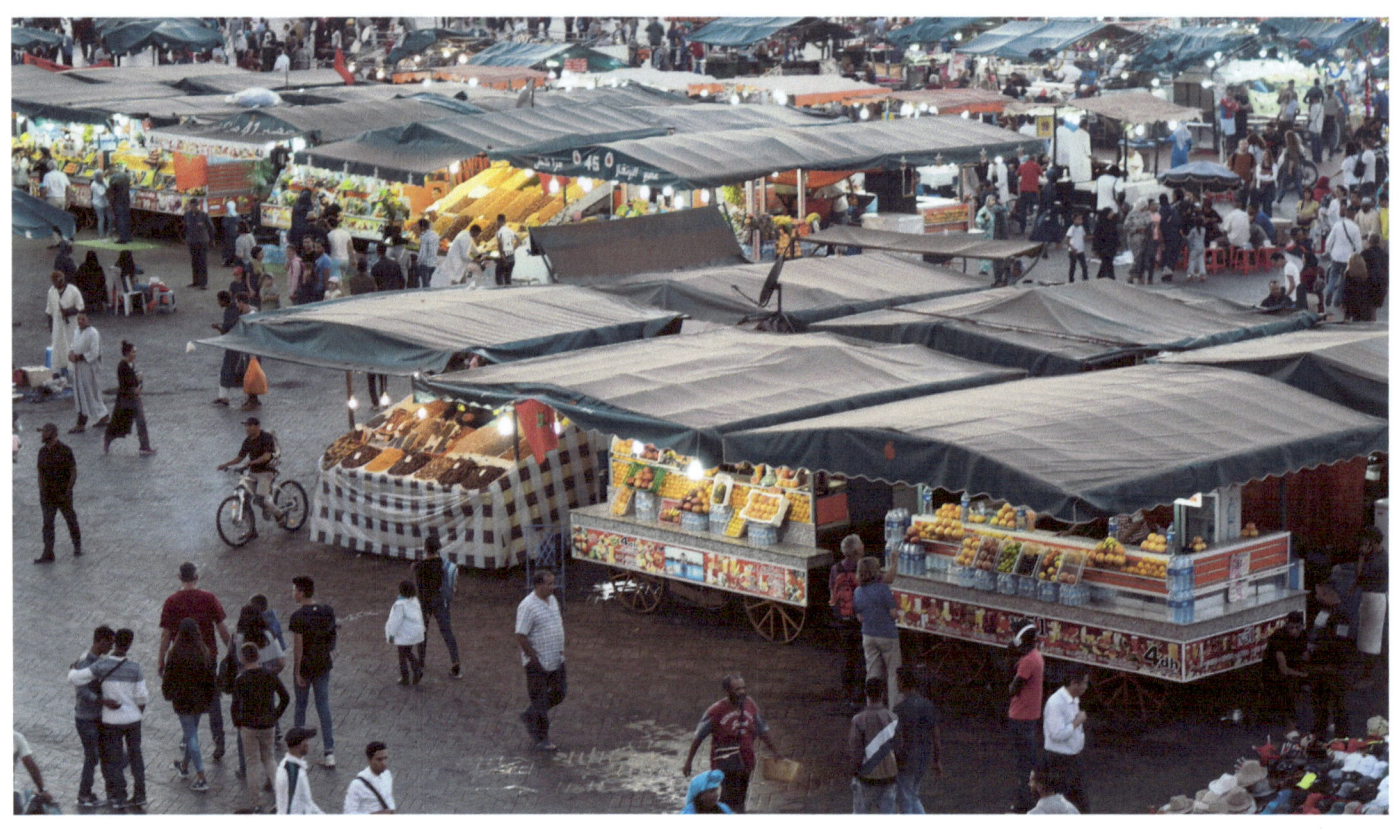

Jemaa el-Fnaa (Arabic: ساحة جامع الفناء *saaHat jamaa' al-fanâ'*, also **Jemaa el-Fna**, **Djema el-Fna** or **Djemaa el-Fnaa**) is a square and market place in Marrakesh's medina quarter (old city). It remains the main square of Marrakesh, used by locals and tourists.

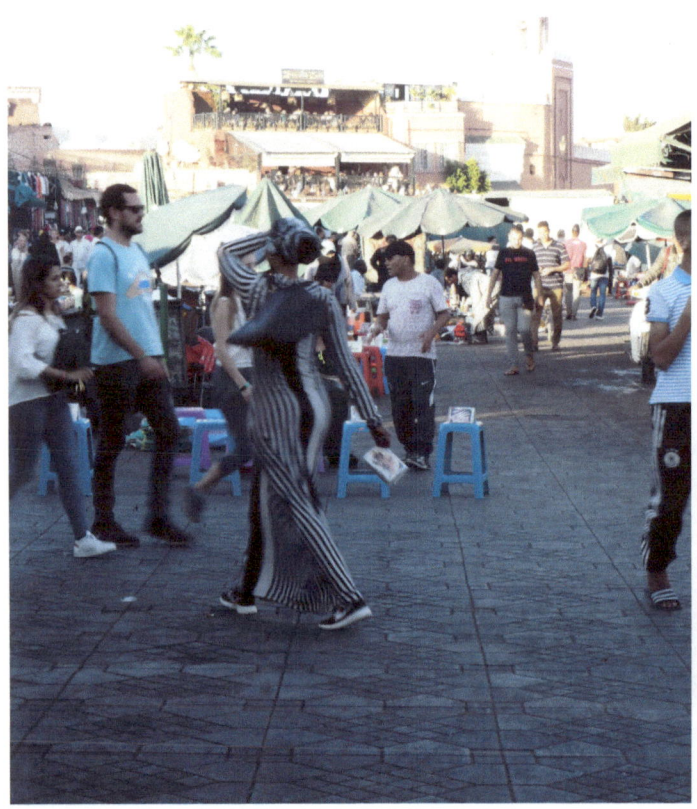
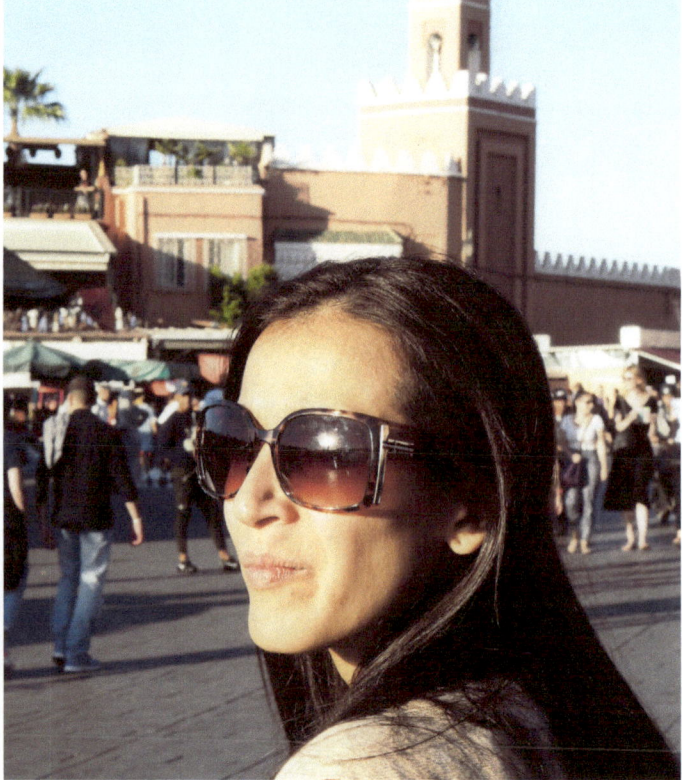

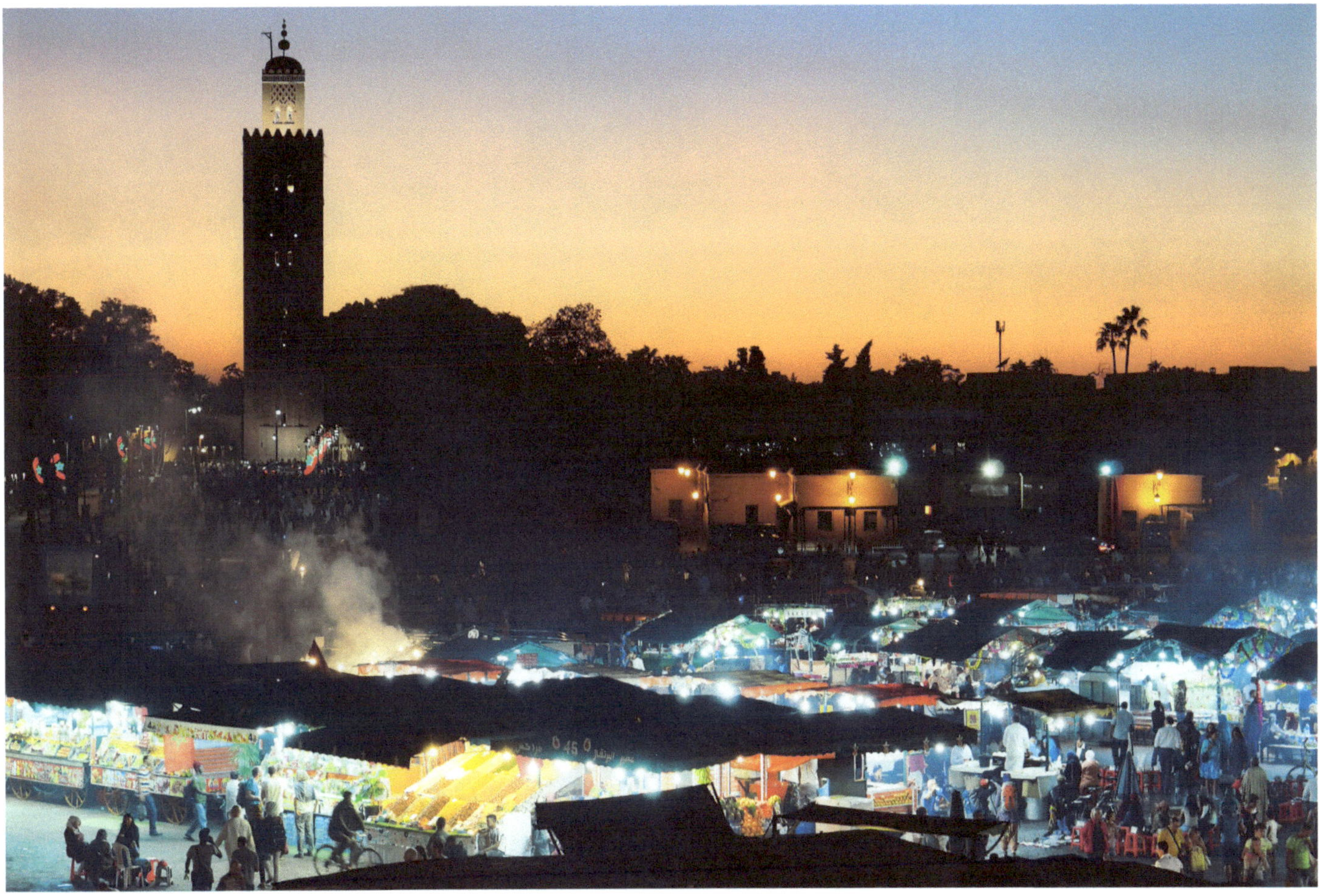

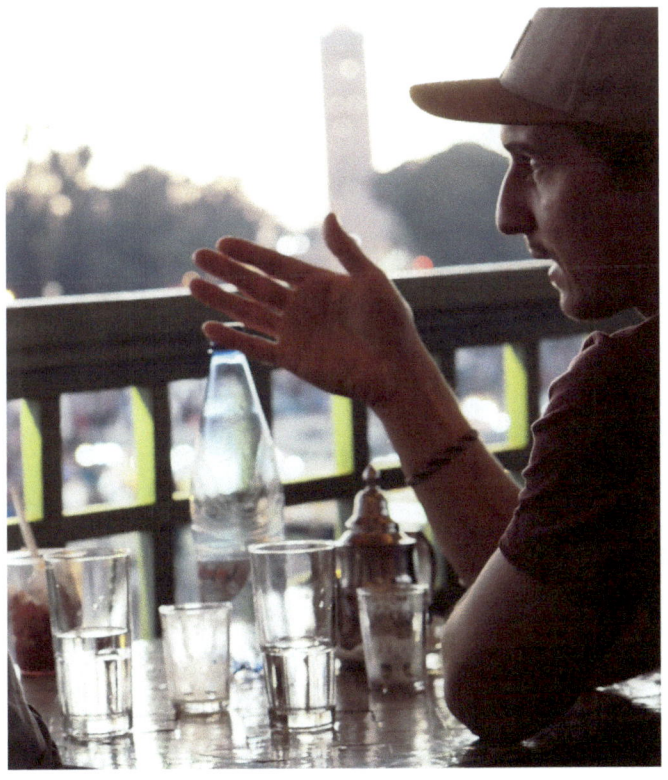

When it gets dark the whole square becomes an open-air restaurant when the stalls start selling street food.

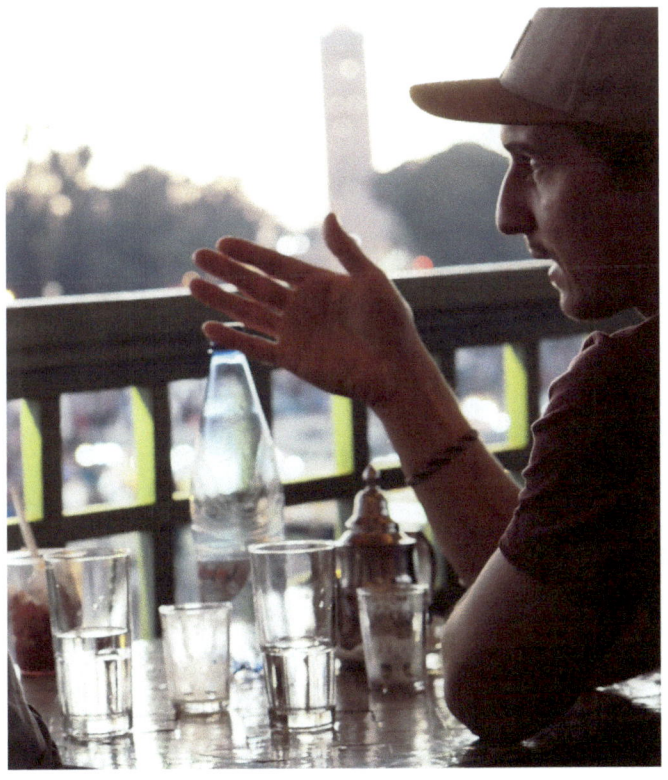

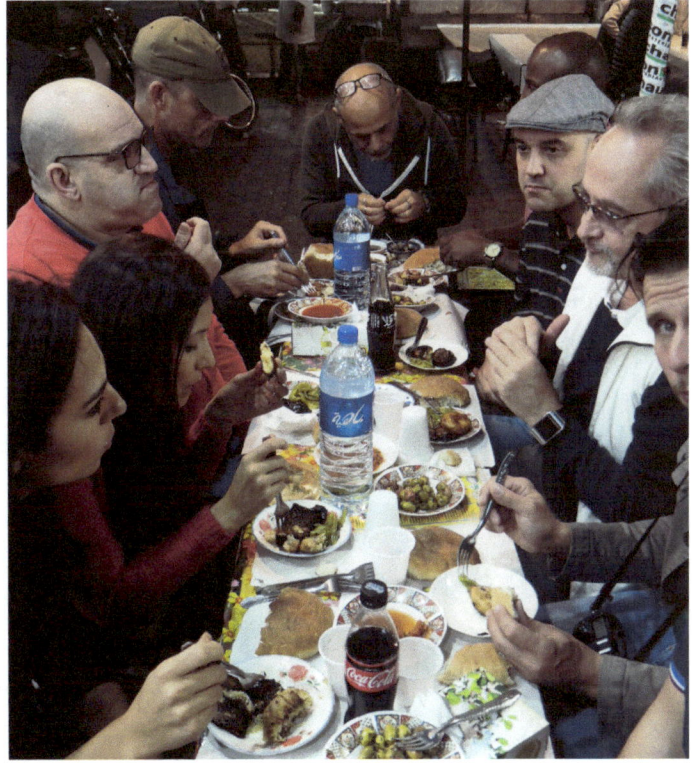

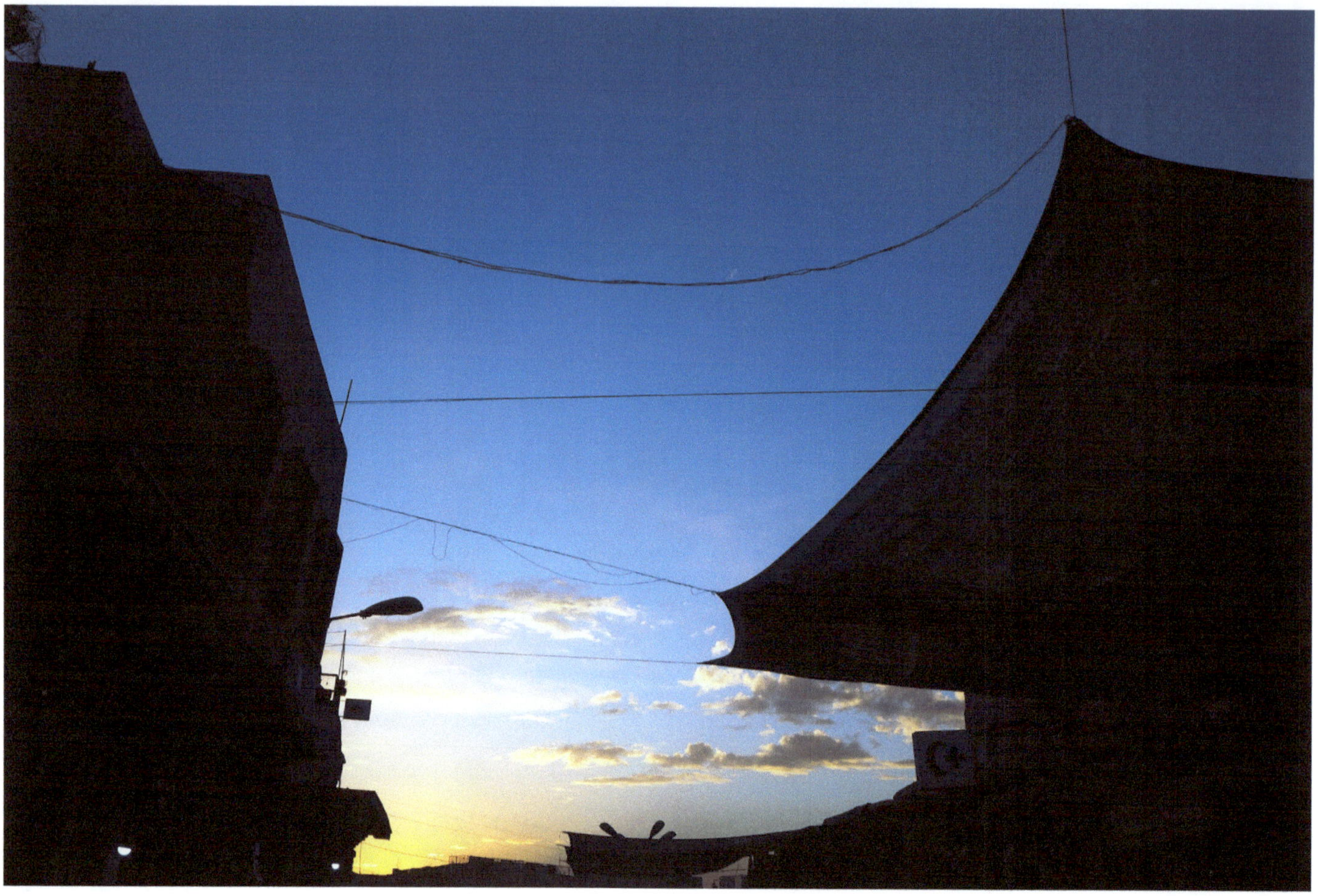

The sunset in the Medina and on the main square.

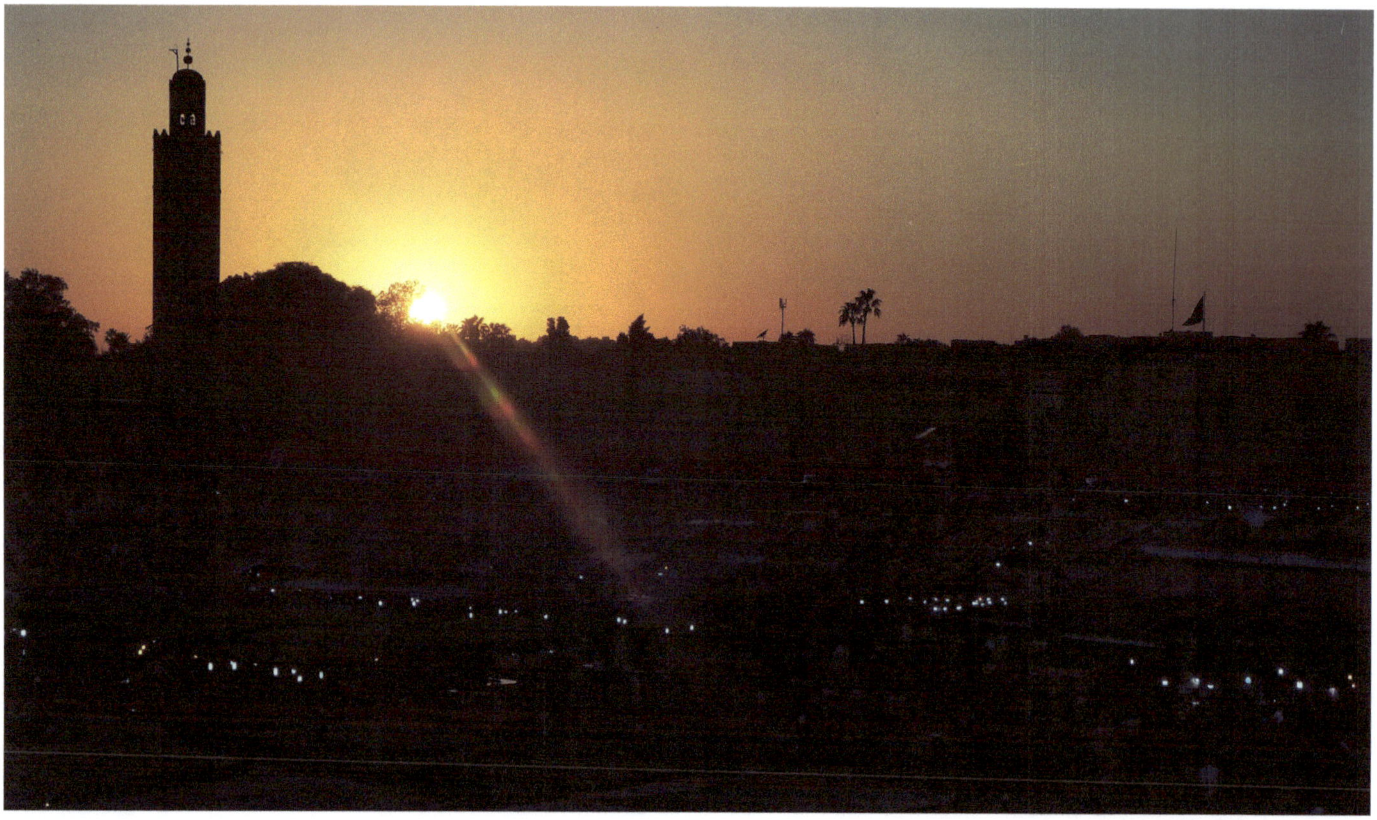

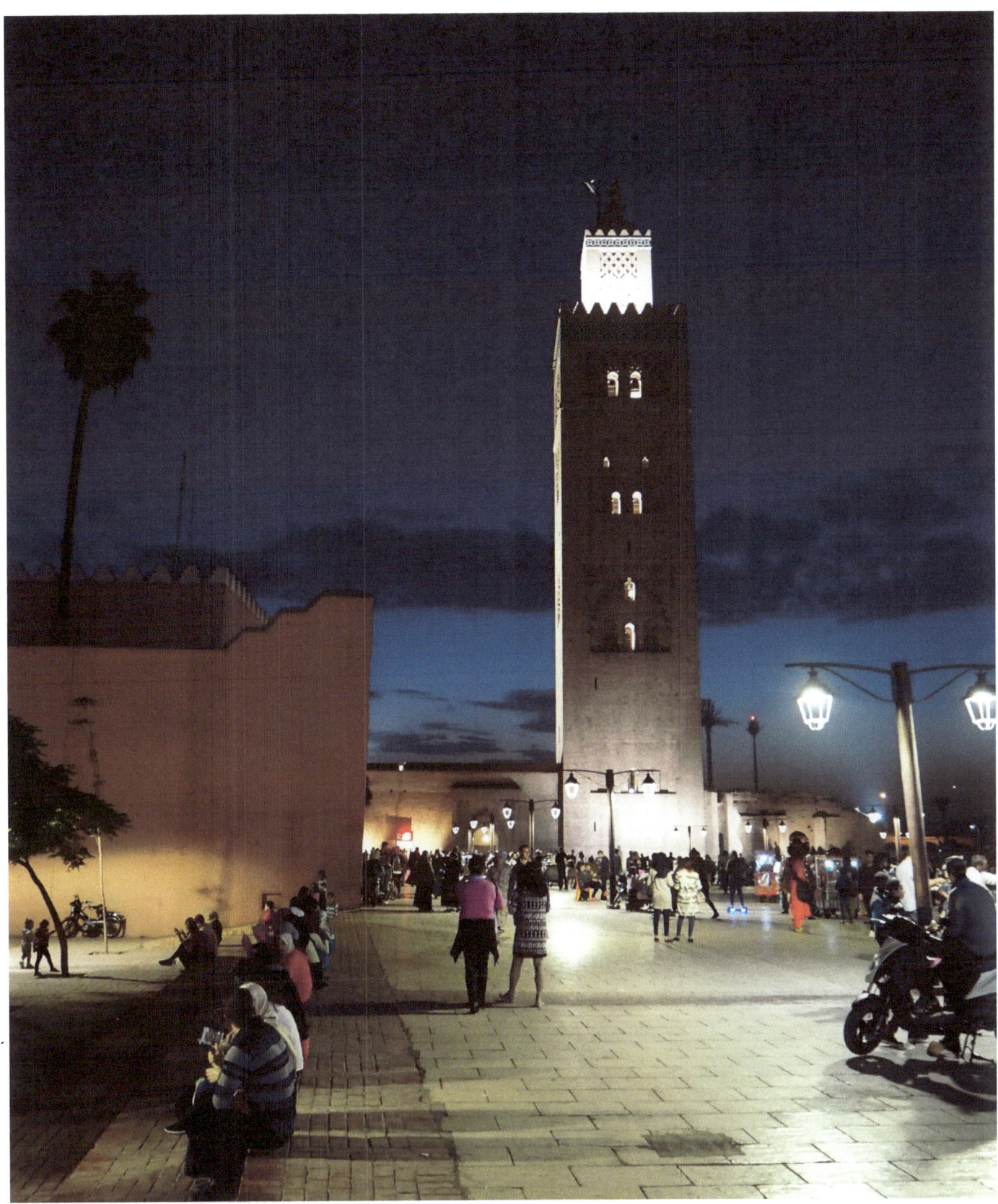

The Koutoubia Mosque or Kutubiyya Mosque (Arabic: جامع الكتبية Arabic pronunciation: [jaːmiʕu‿lkutubijːa(h)]) is the largest mosque in Marrakesh, Morocco.

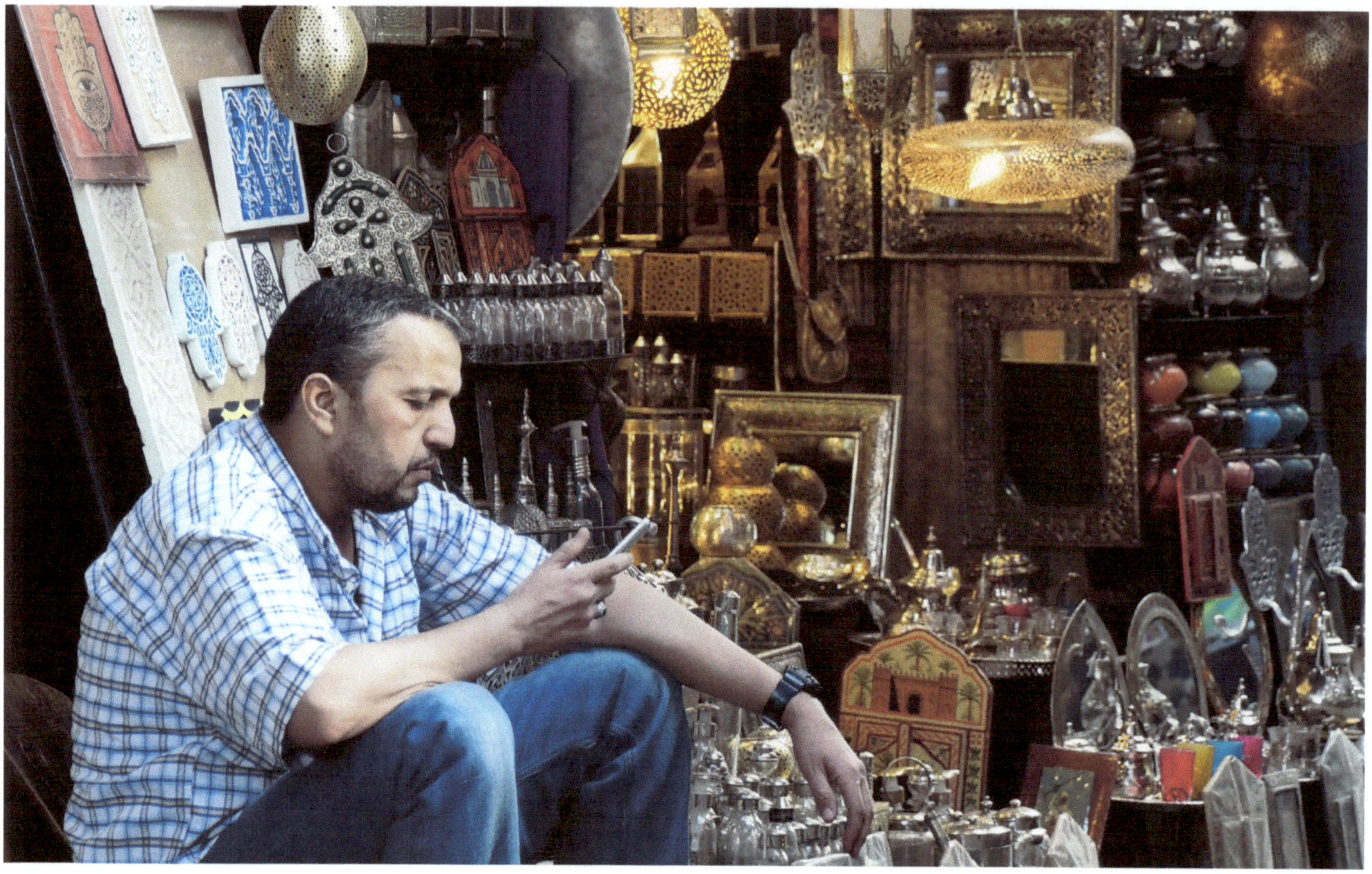

Everyday life in the streets of Marrakech

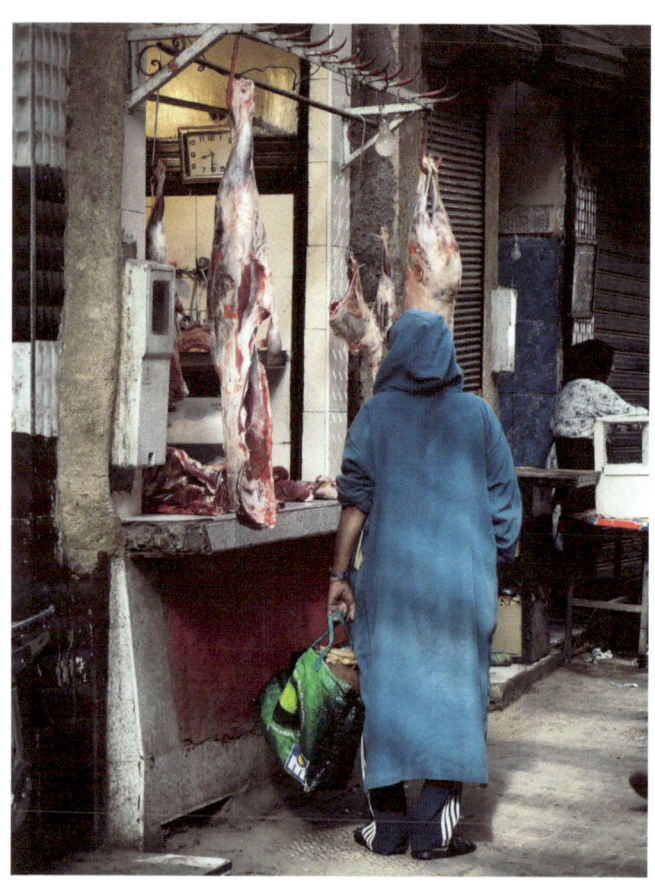

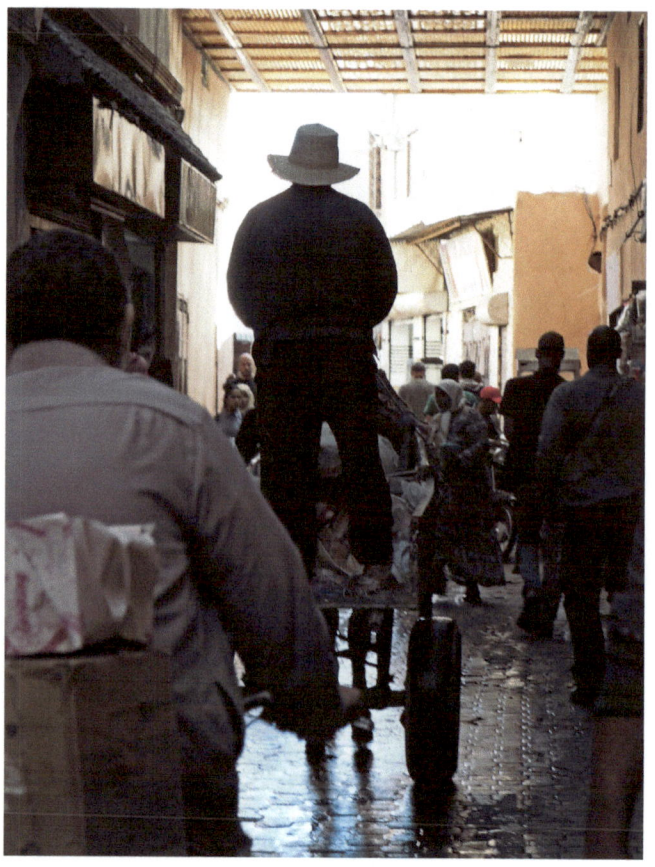

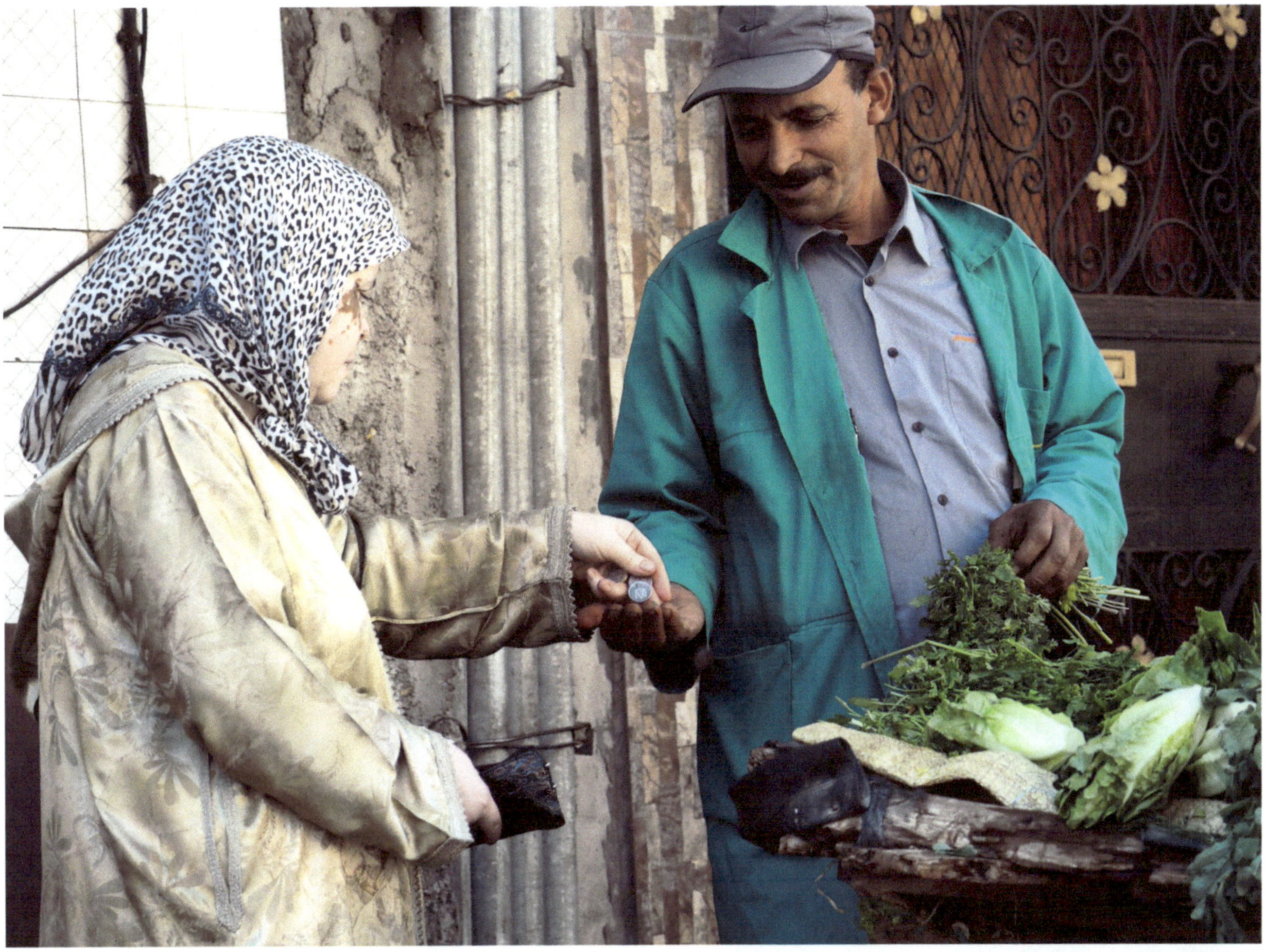

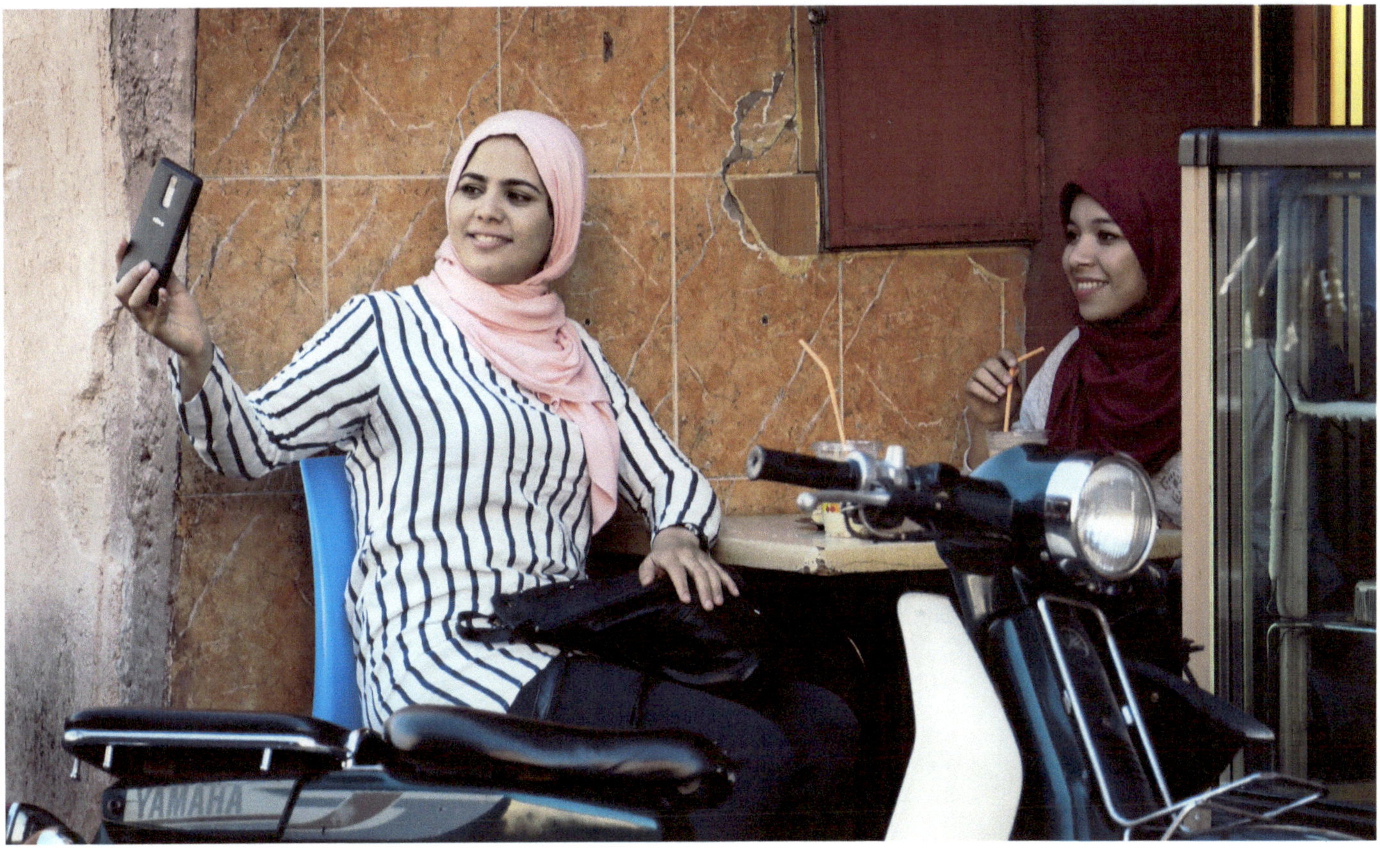
YAMAHA

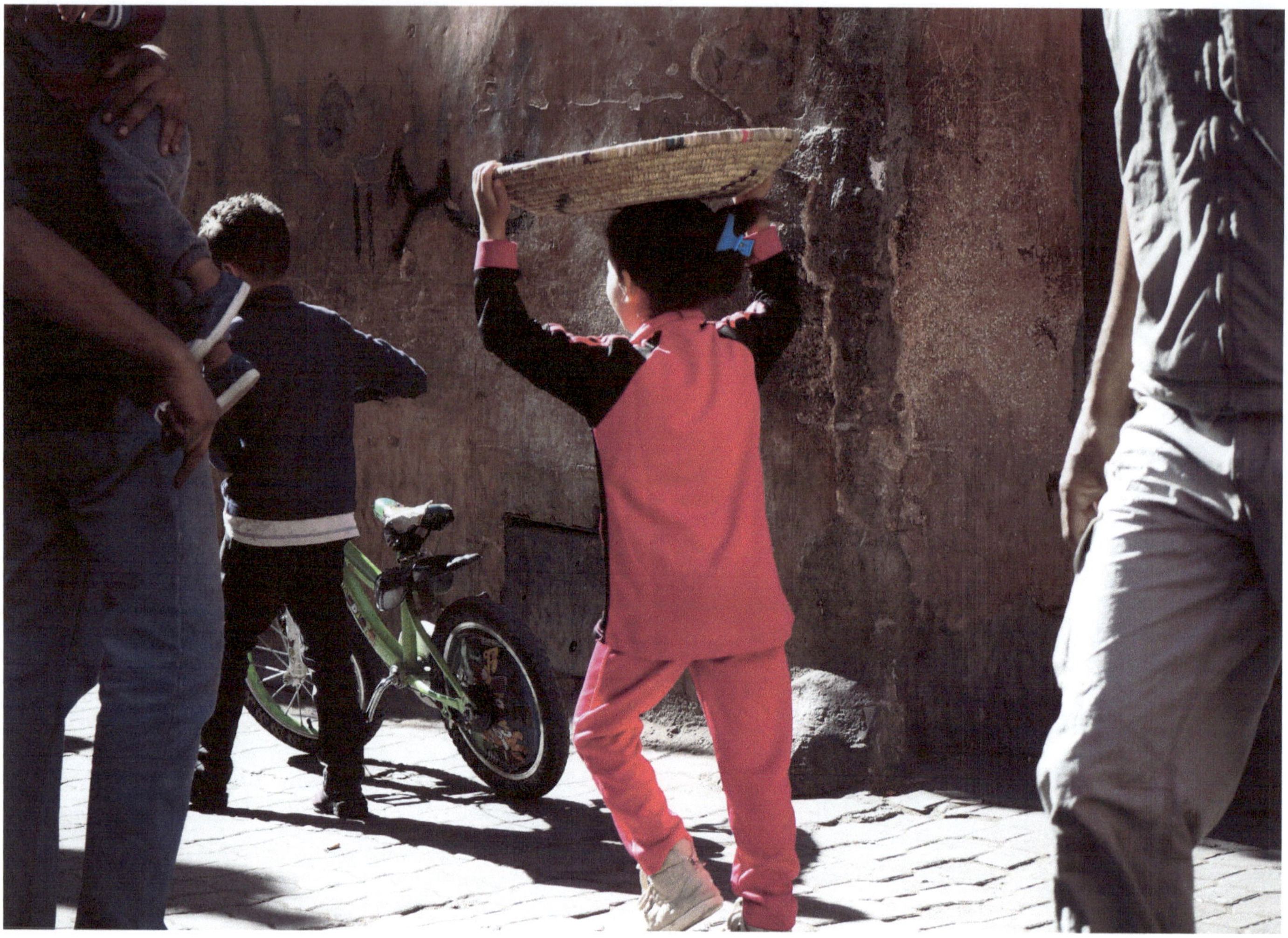

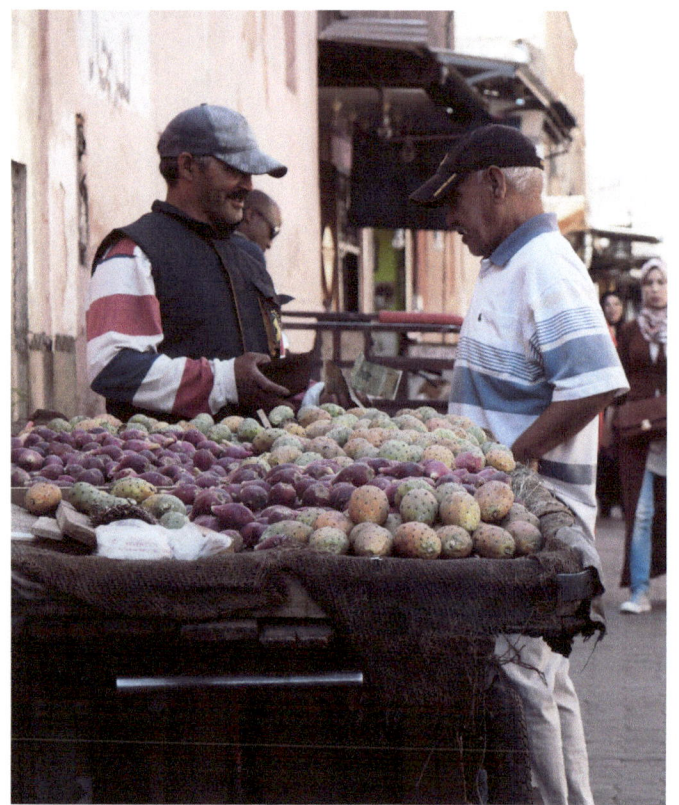

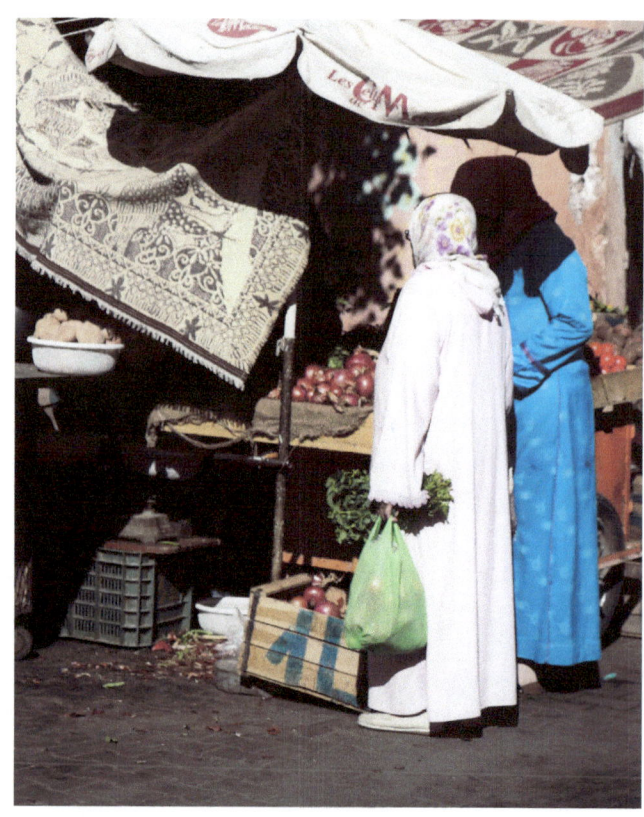

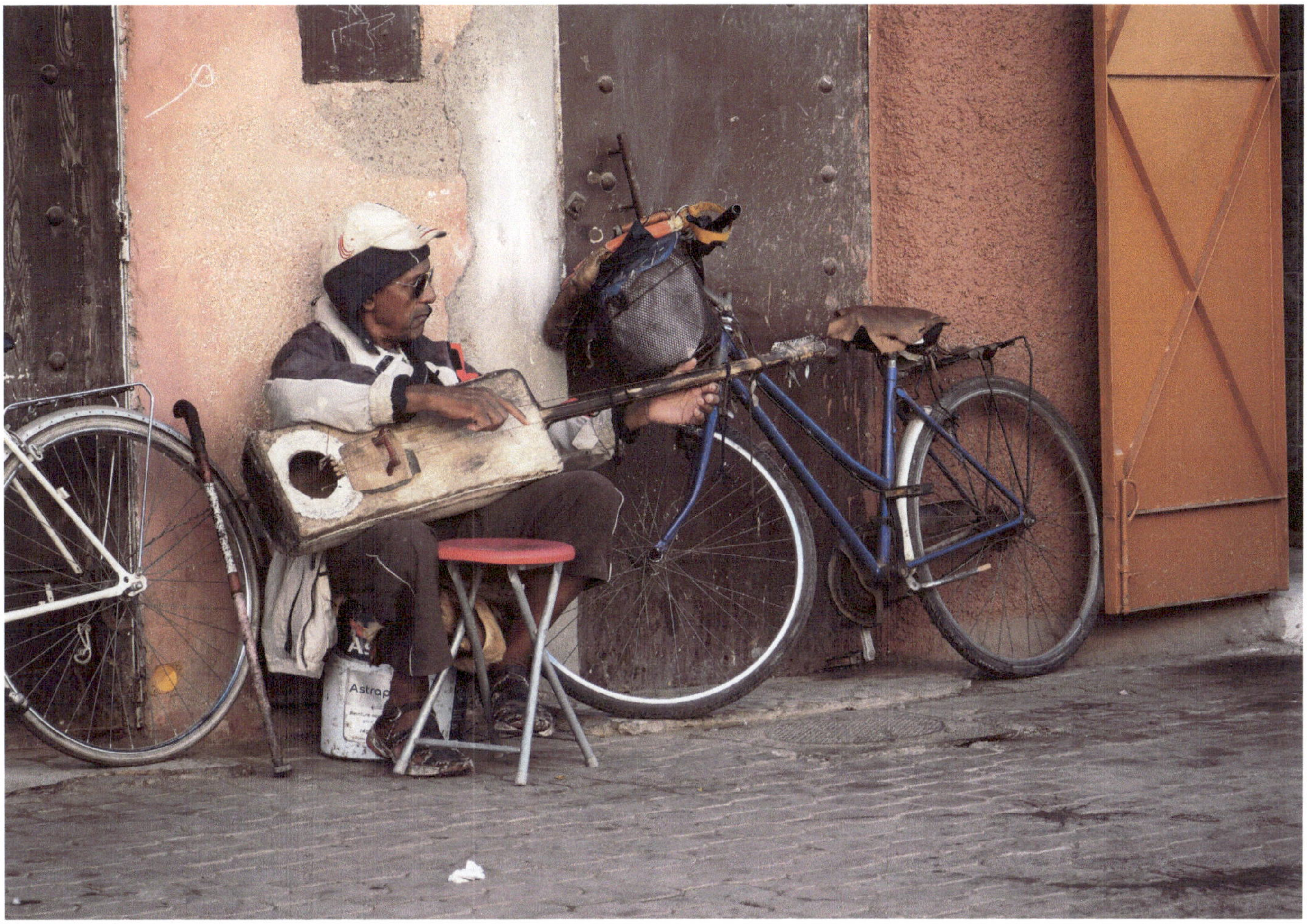

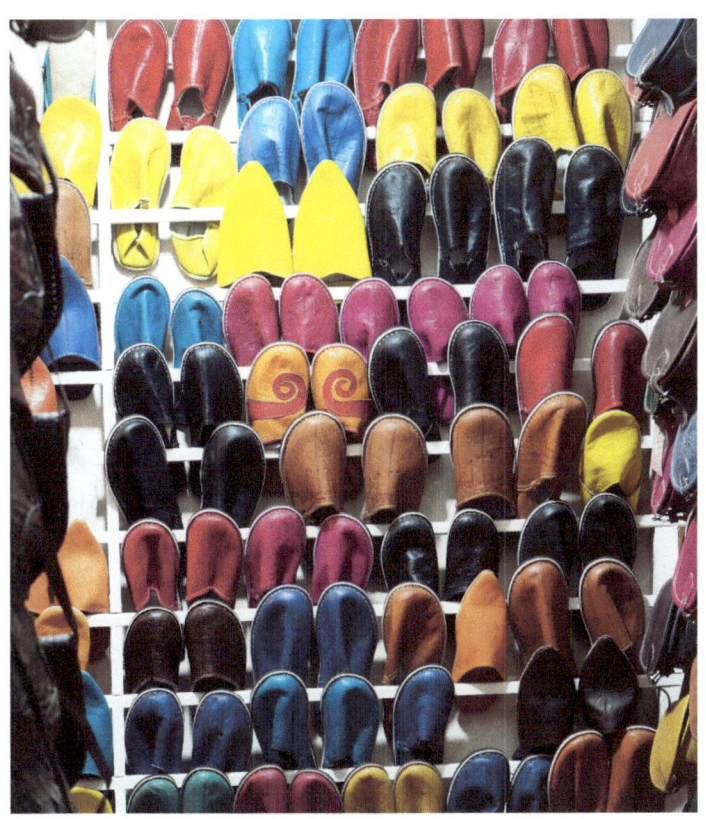
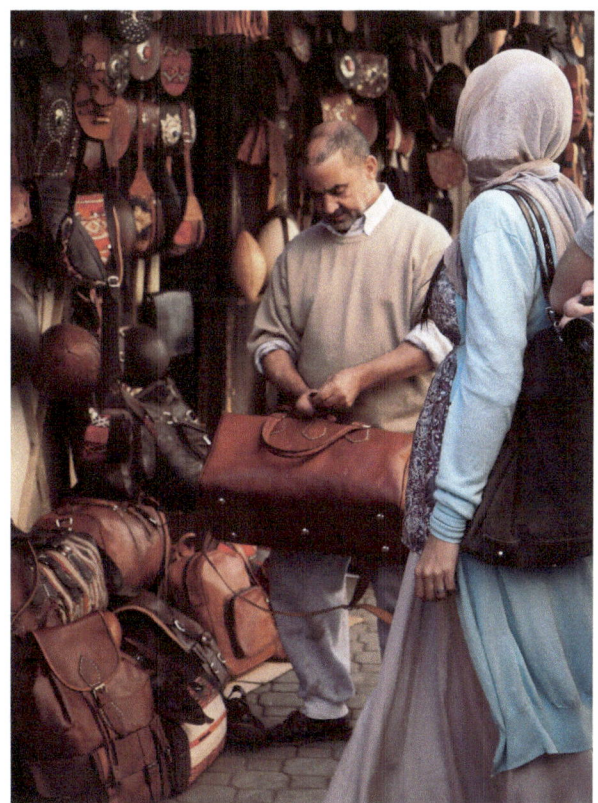

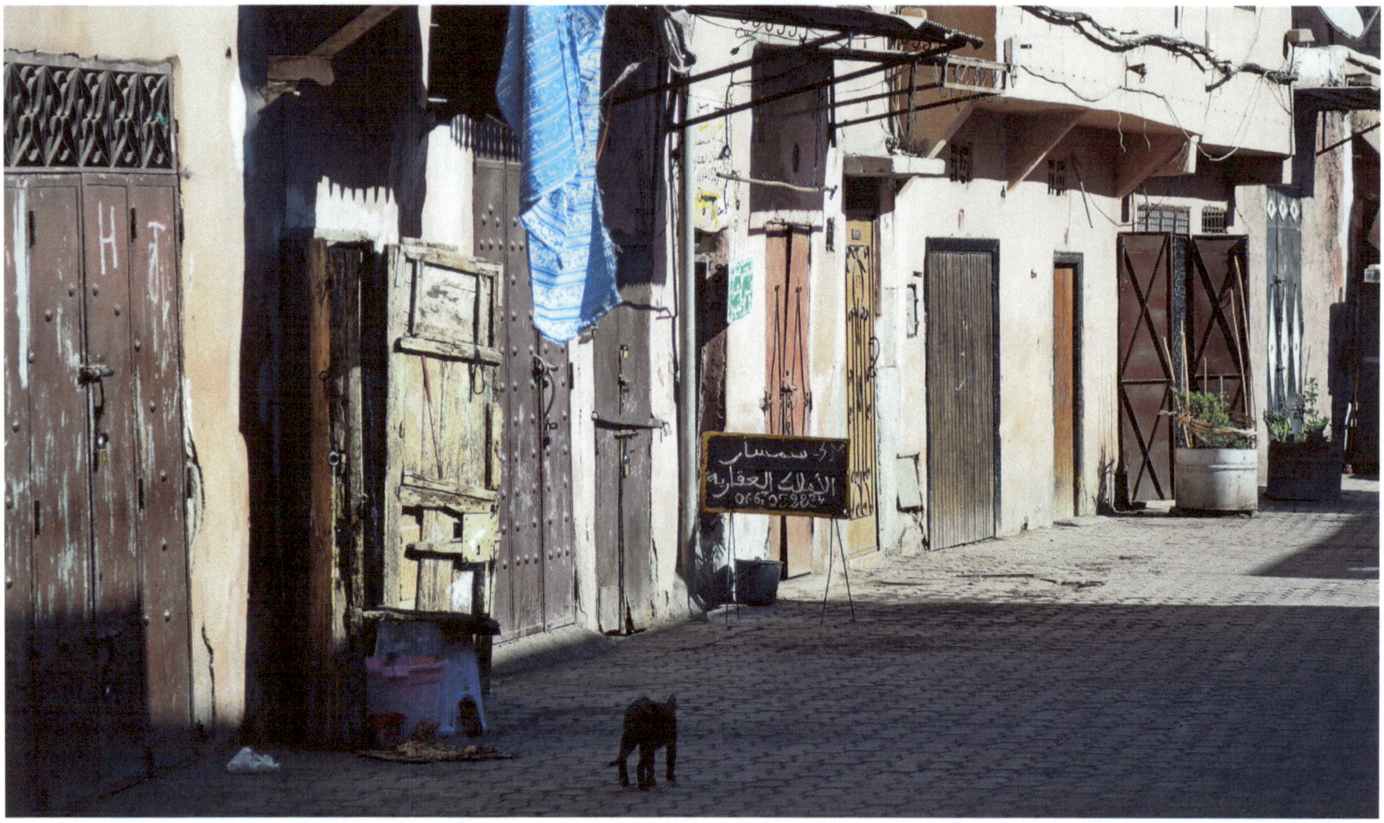

In the hottest hours of the day the city is almost deserted

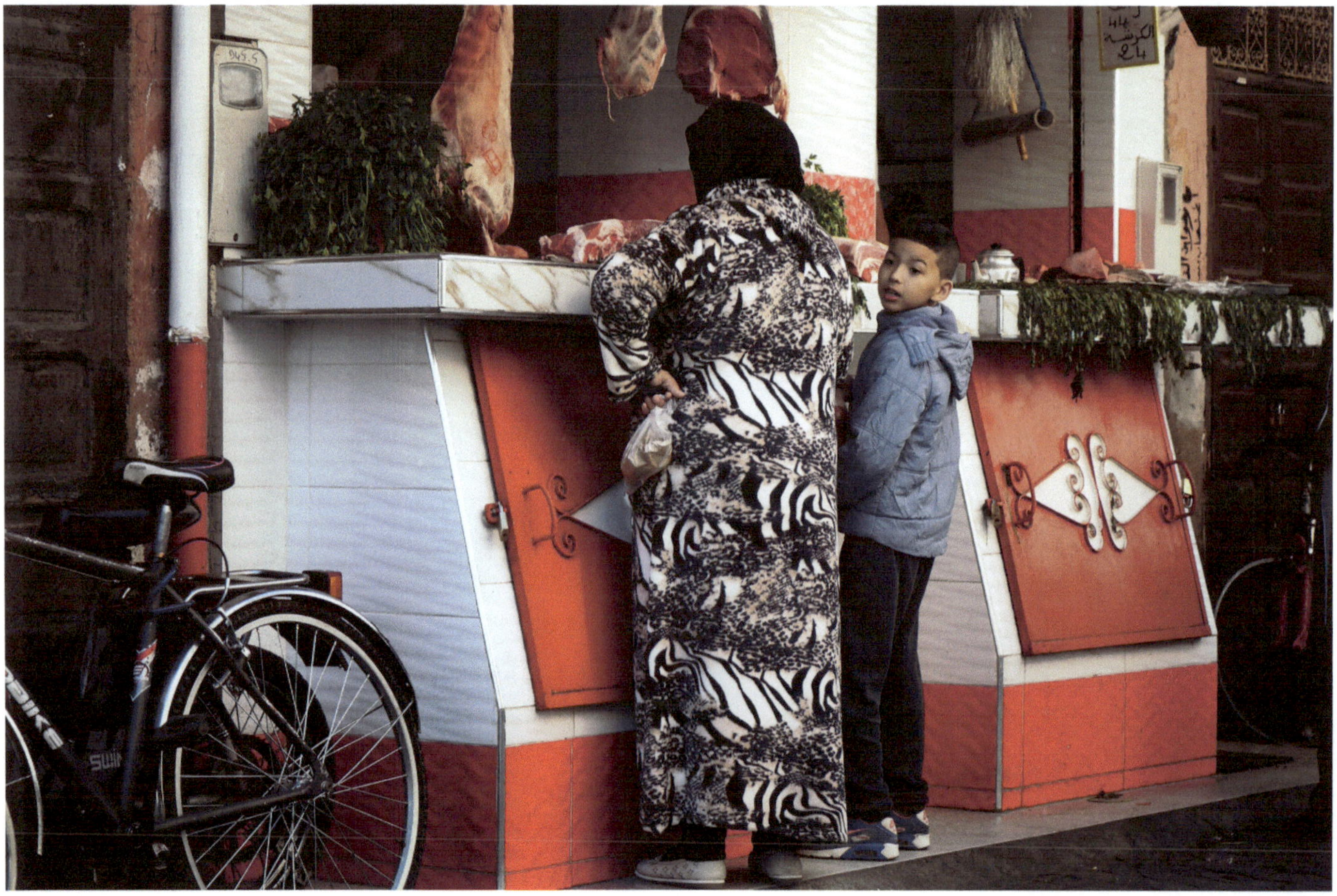

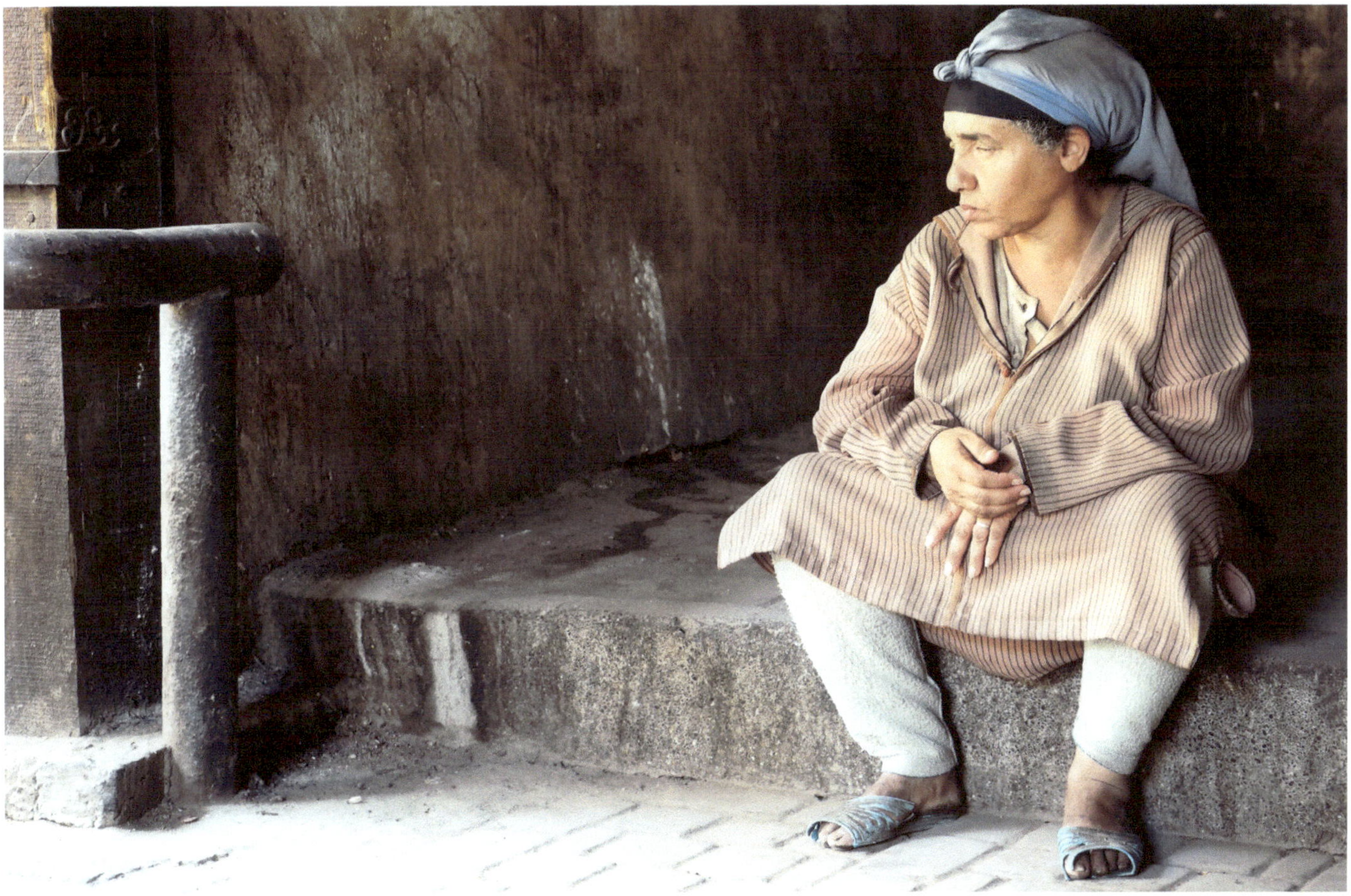

Even if the city flourishes with activity and commerce, there is also a lot of visible poverty in the streets.

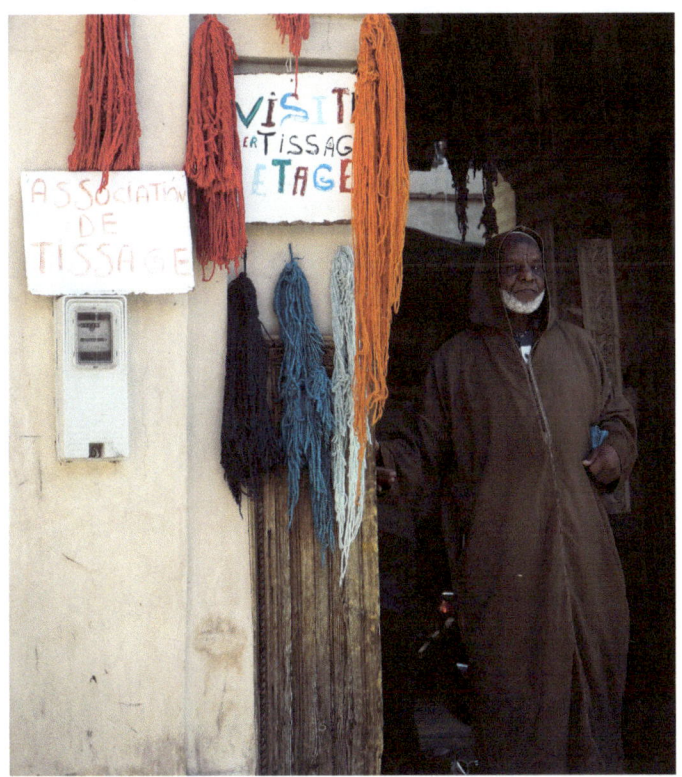

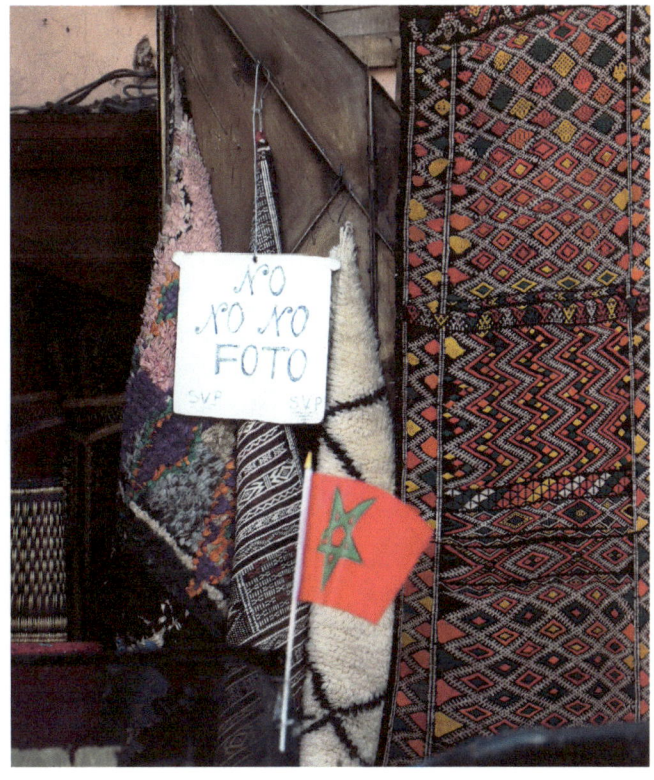

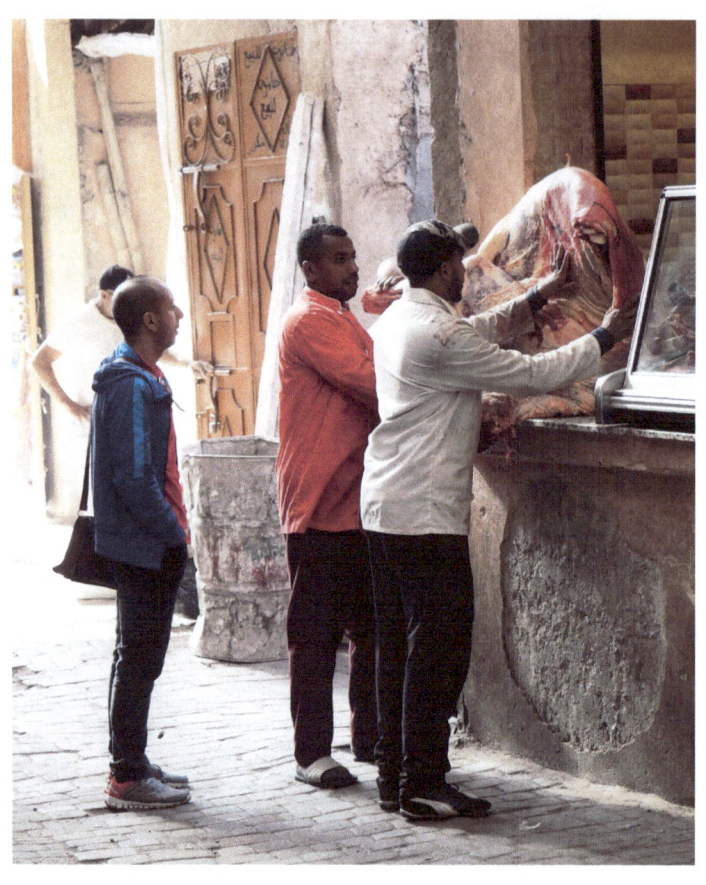 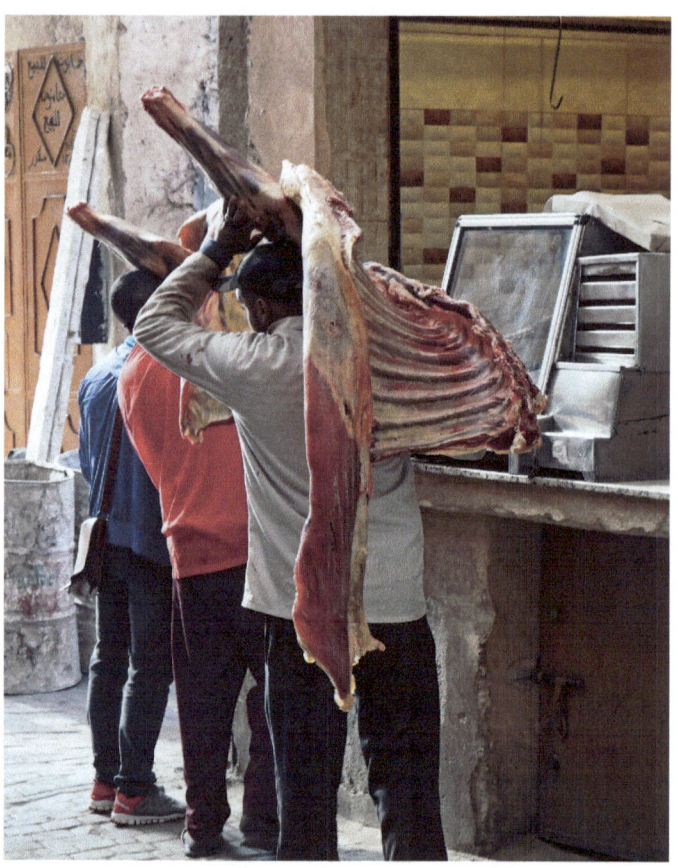

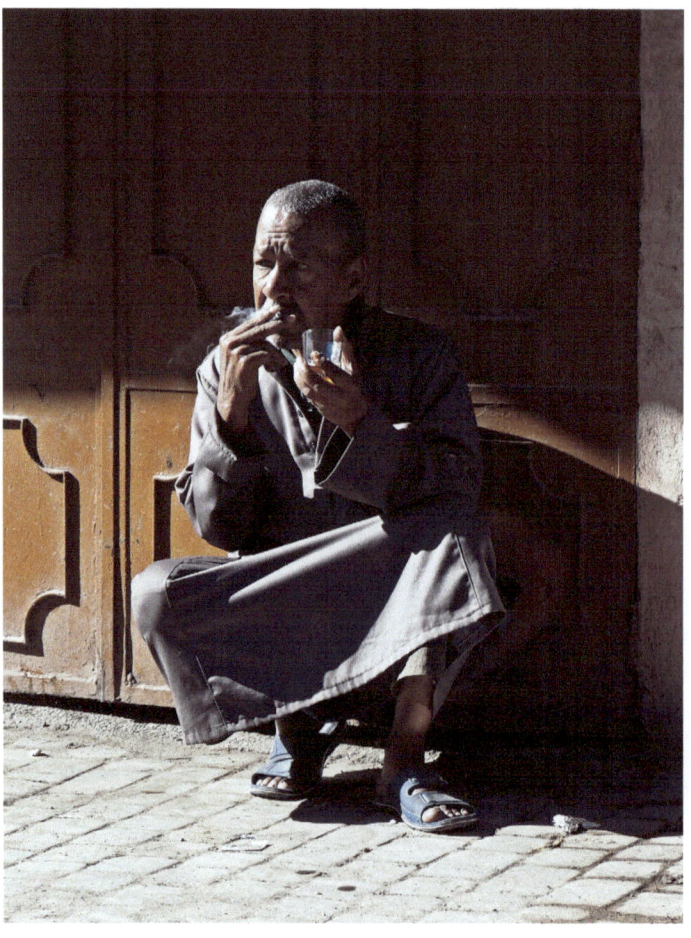 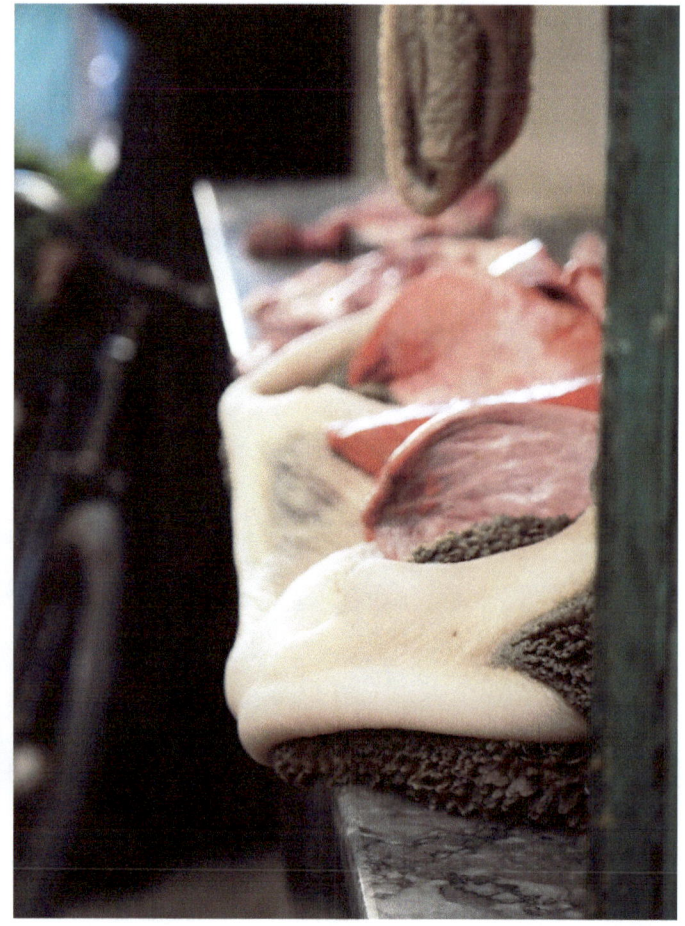

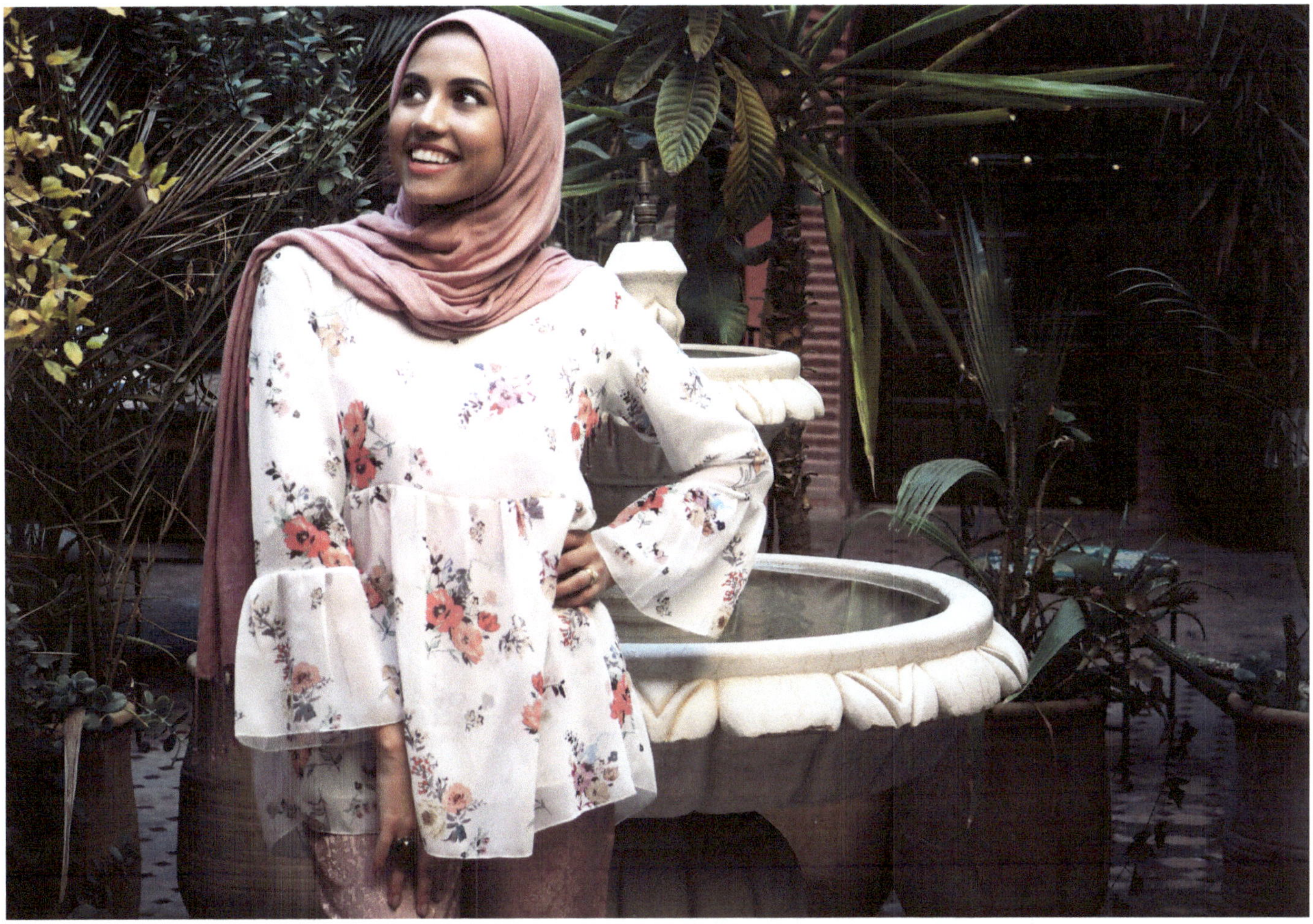

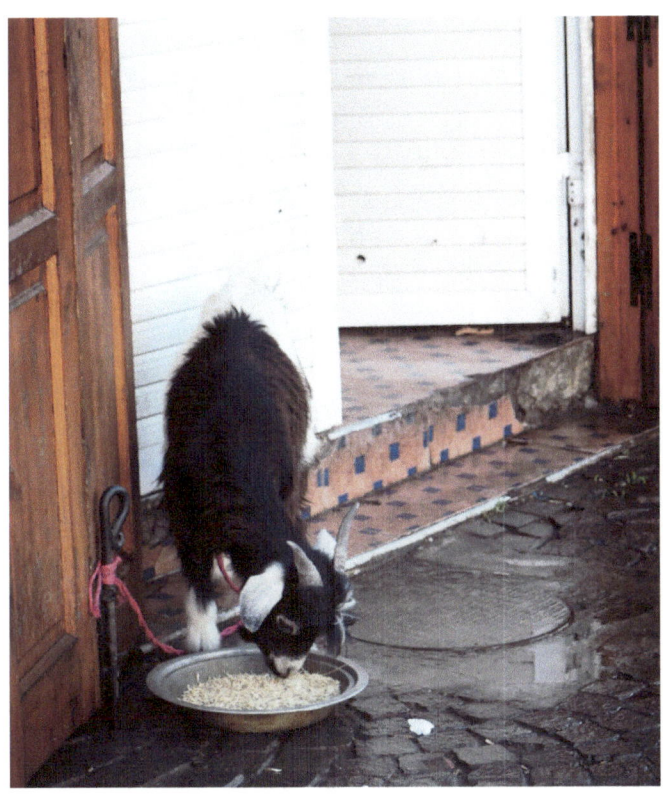

A gorgeous Moroccan girl agrees to pose for us.

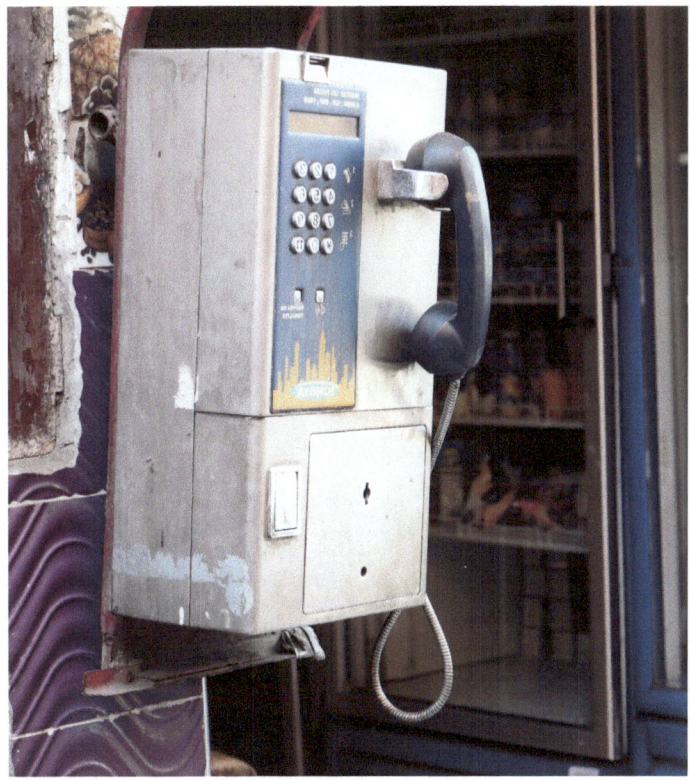

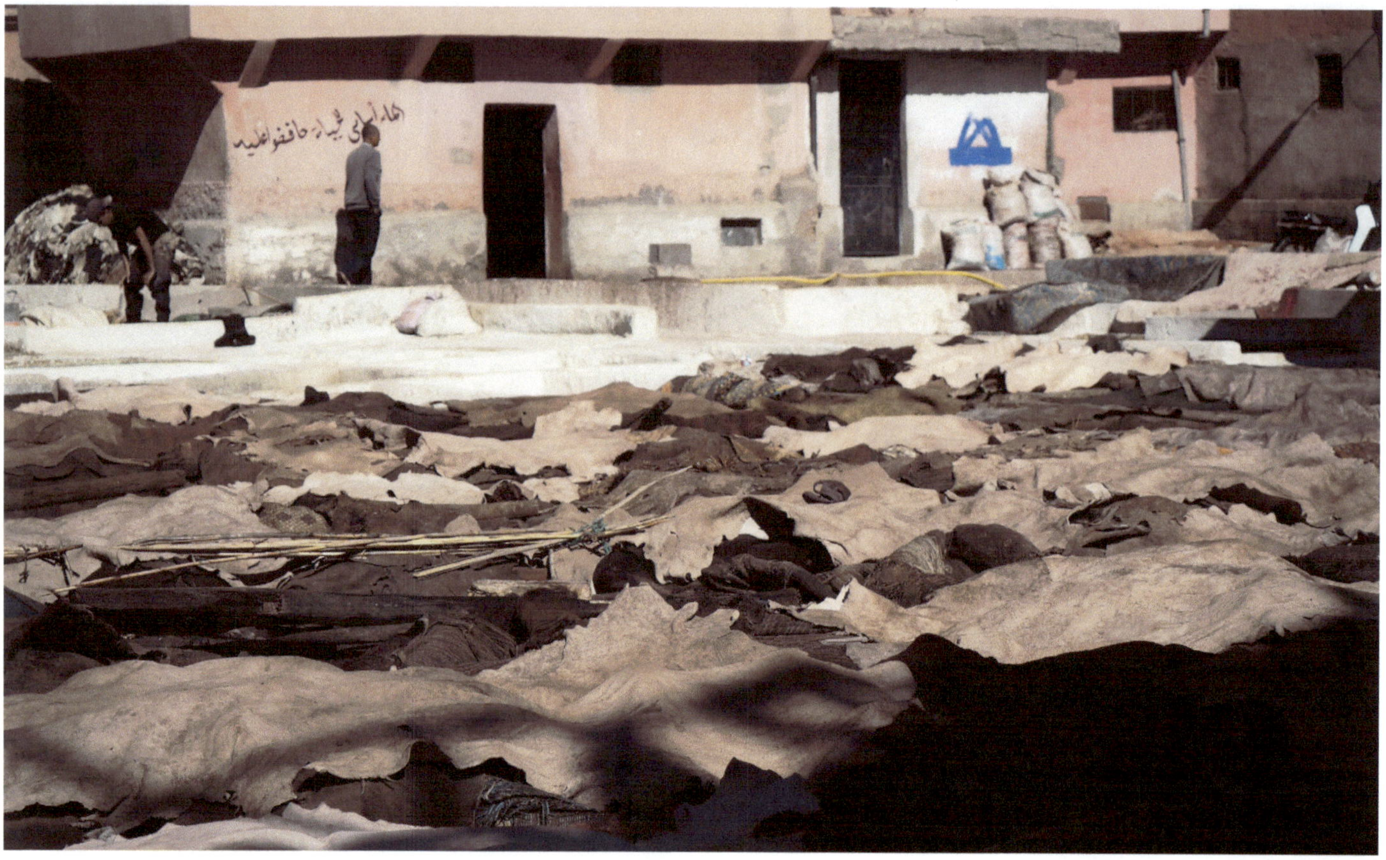

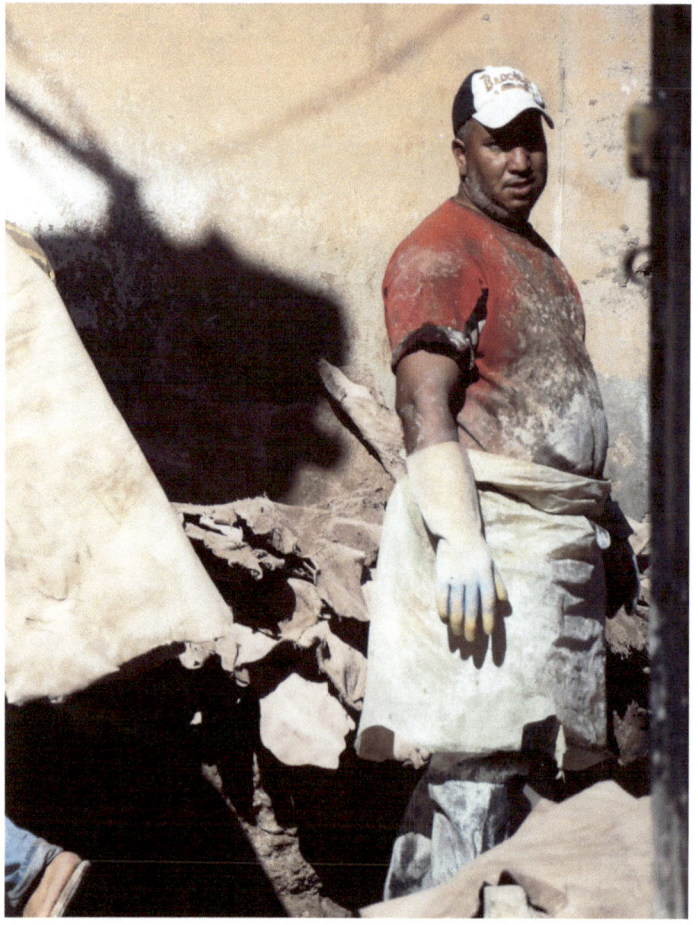
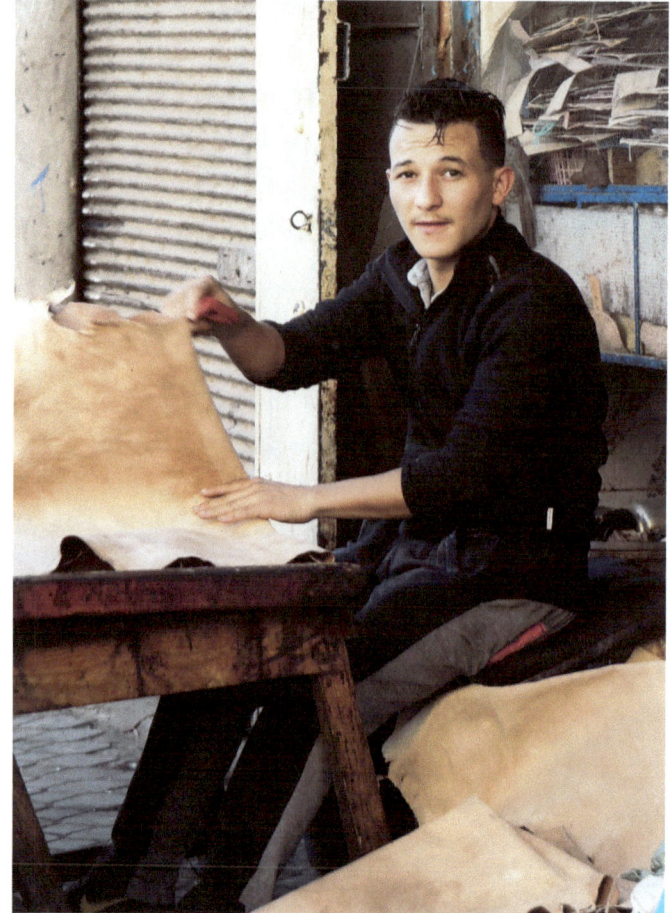

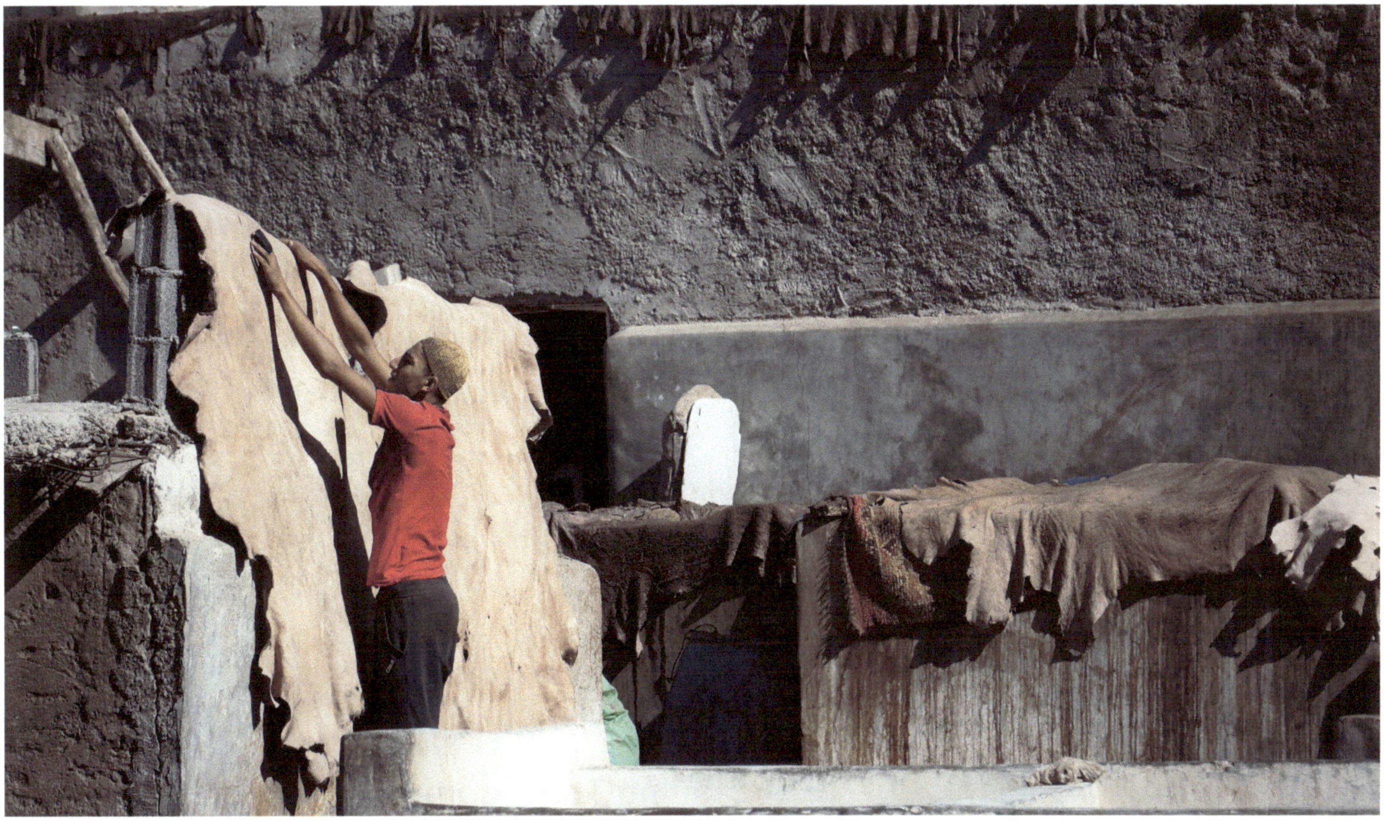

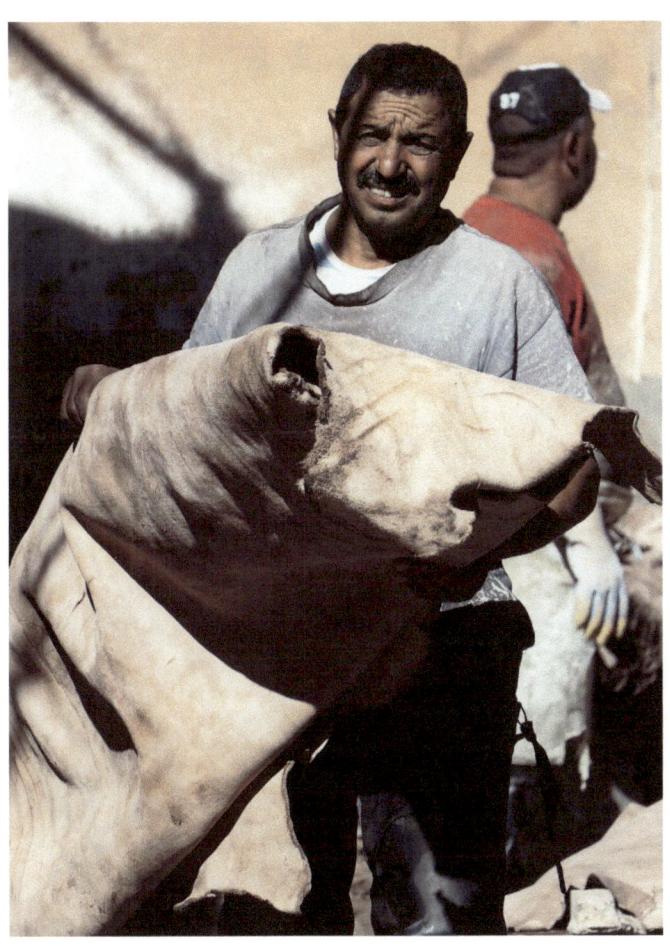

an entire district of Marrakech is occupied by tanneries in open air

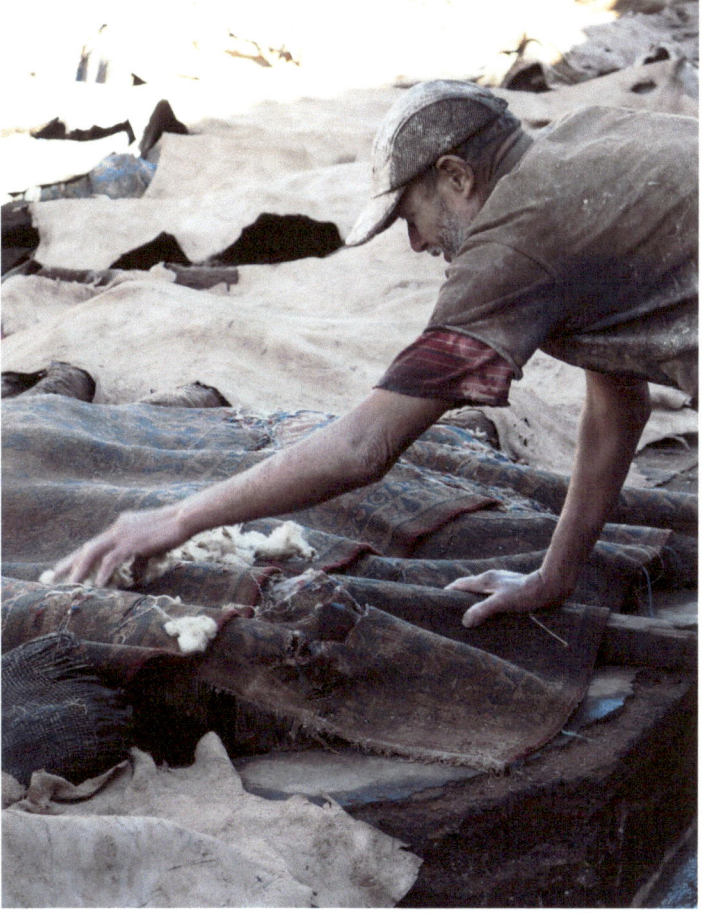

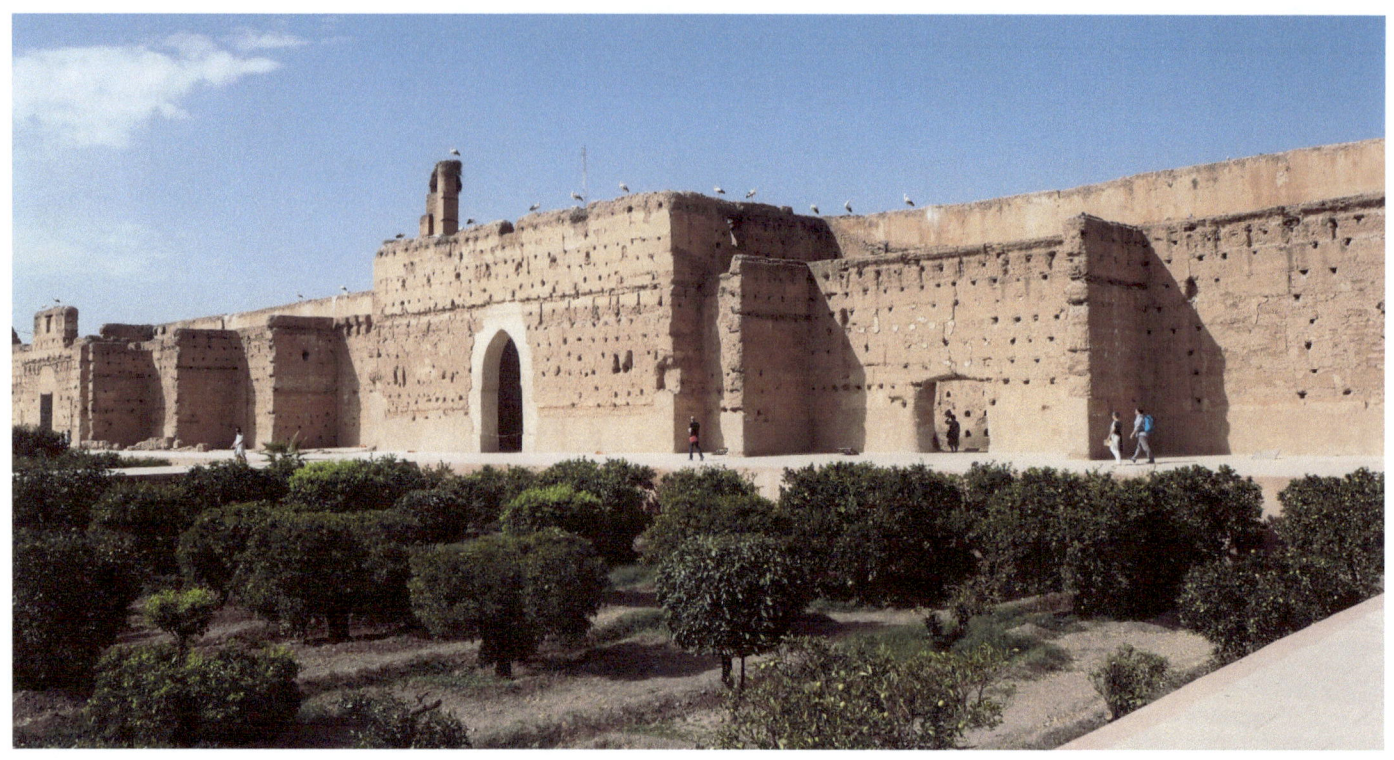

El Badi Palace (Arabic: قصر البديع; meaning The incomparable palace) is a ruined palace. It was commissioned by the sultan Ahmad al-Mansur of the Saadian dynasty sometime shortly after his accession in 1578.

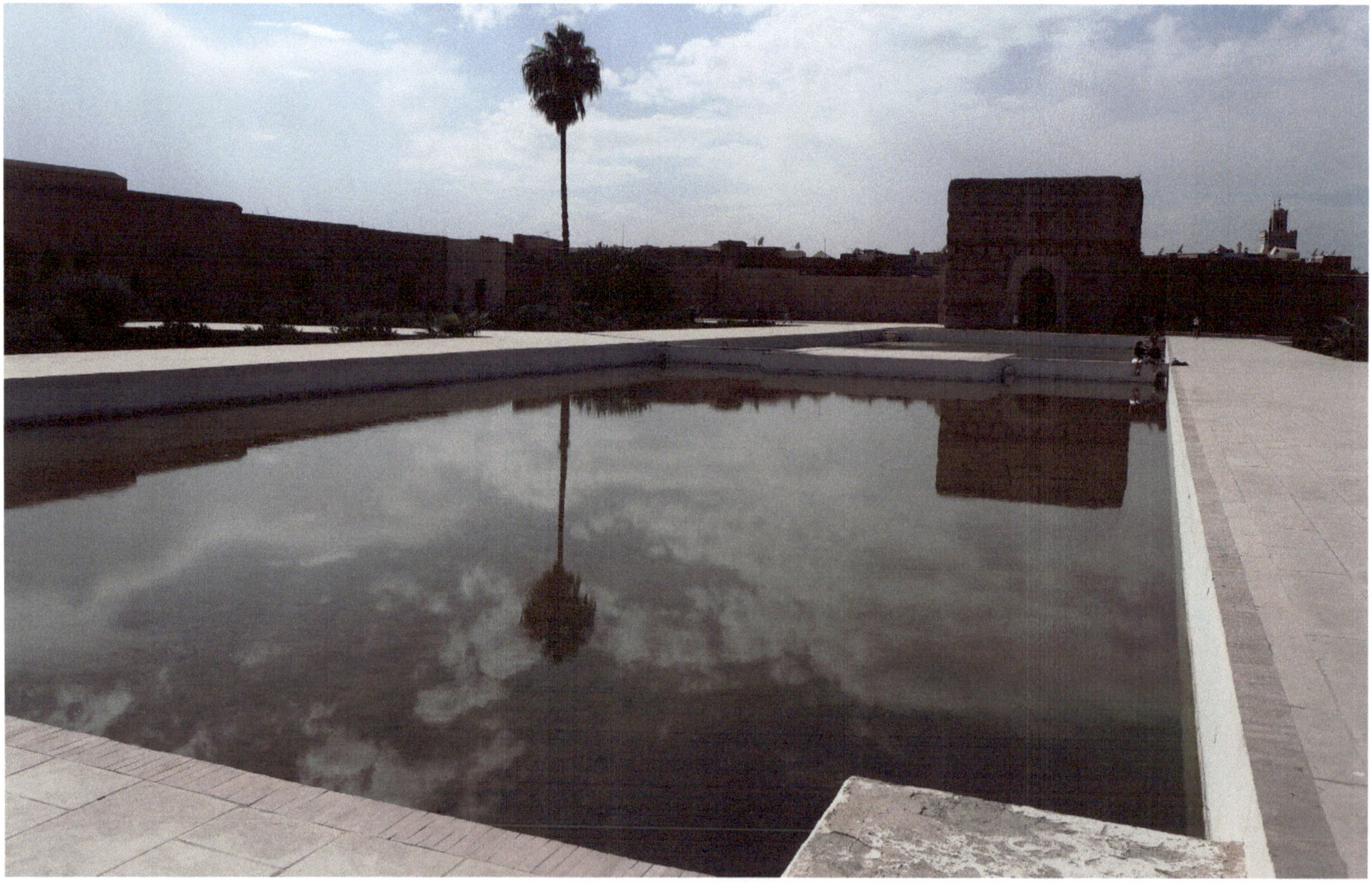

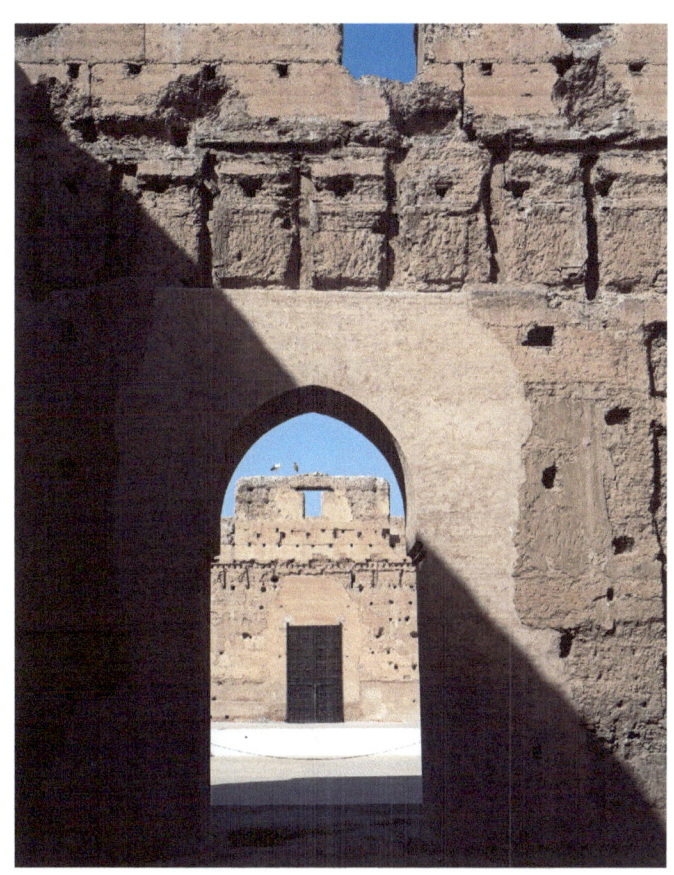

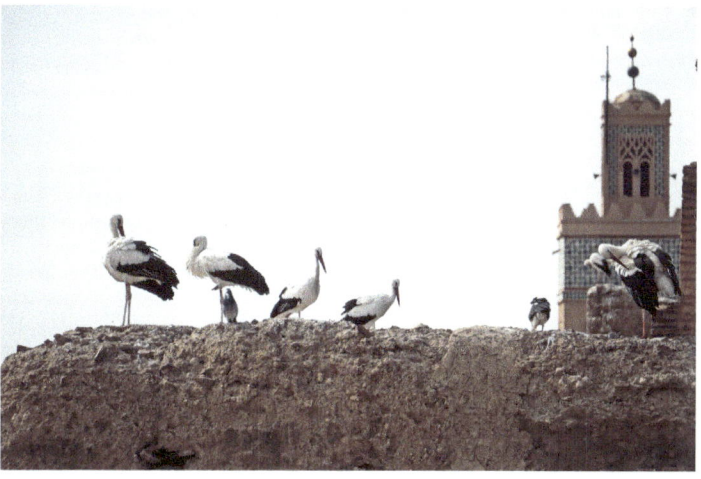

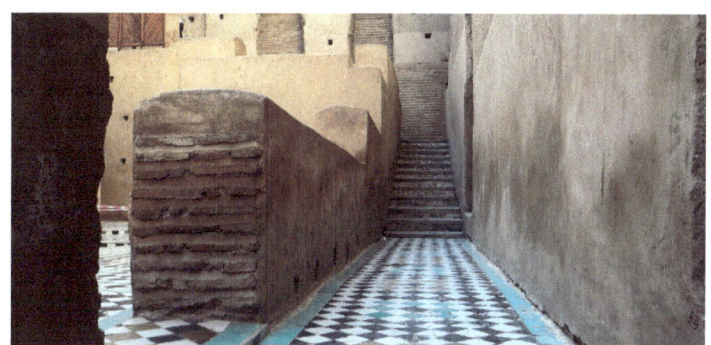

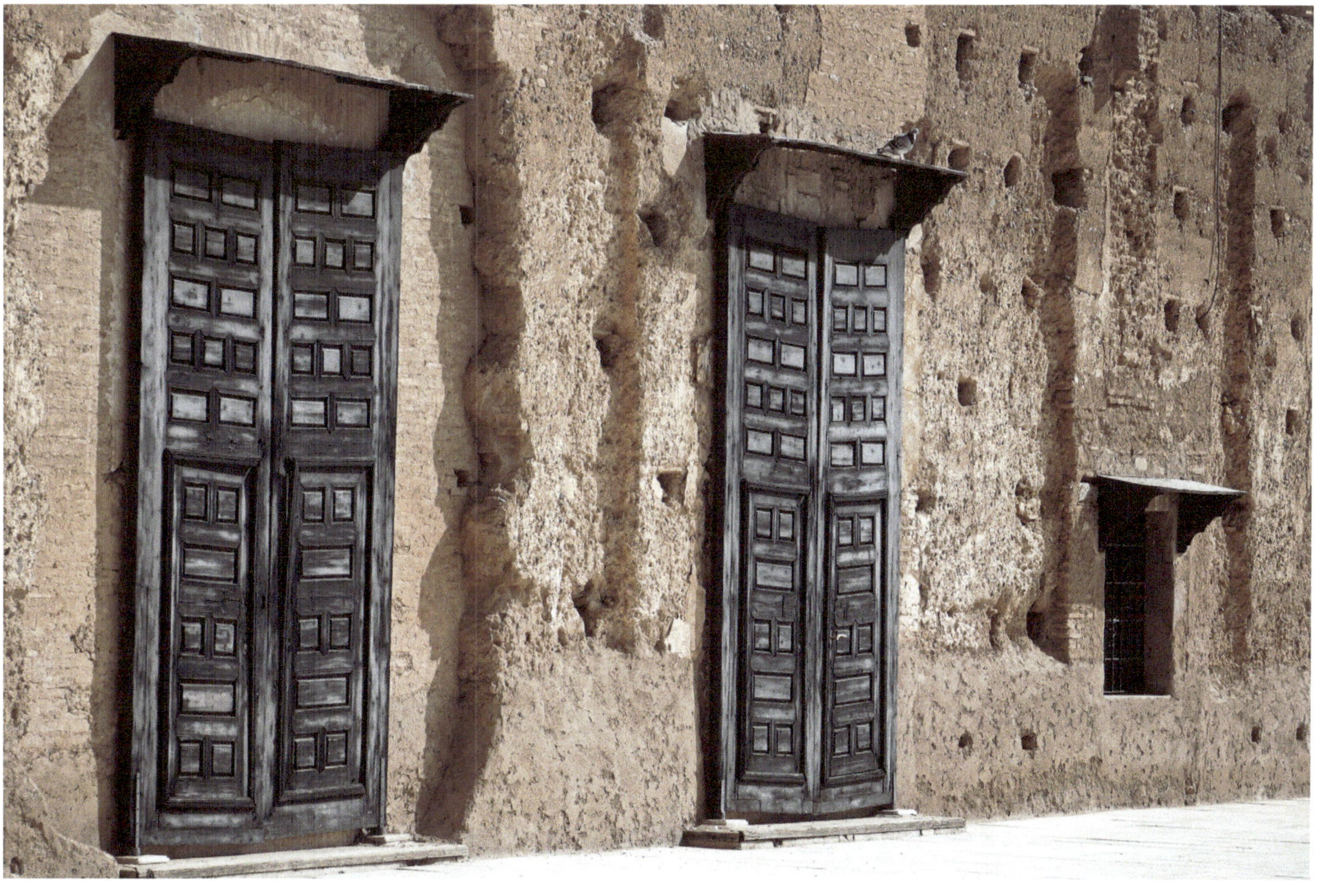

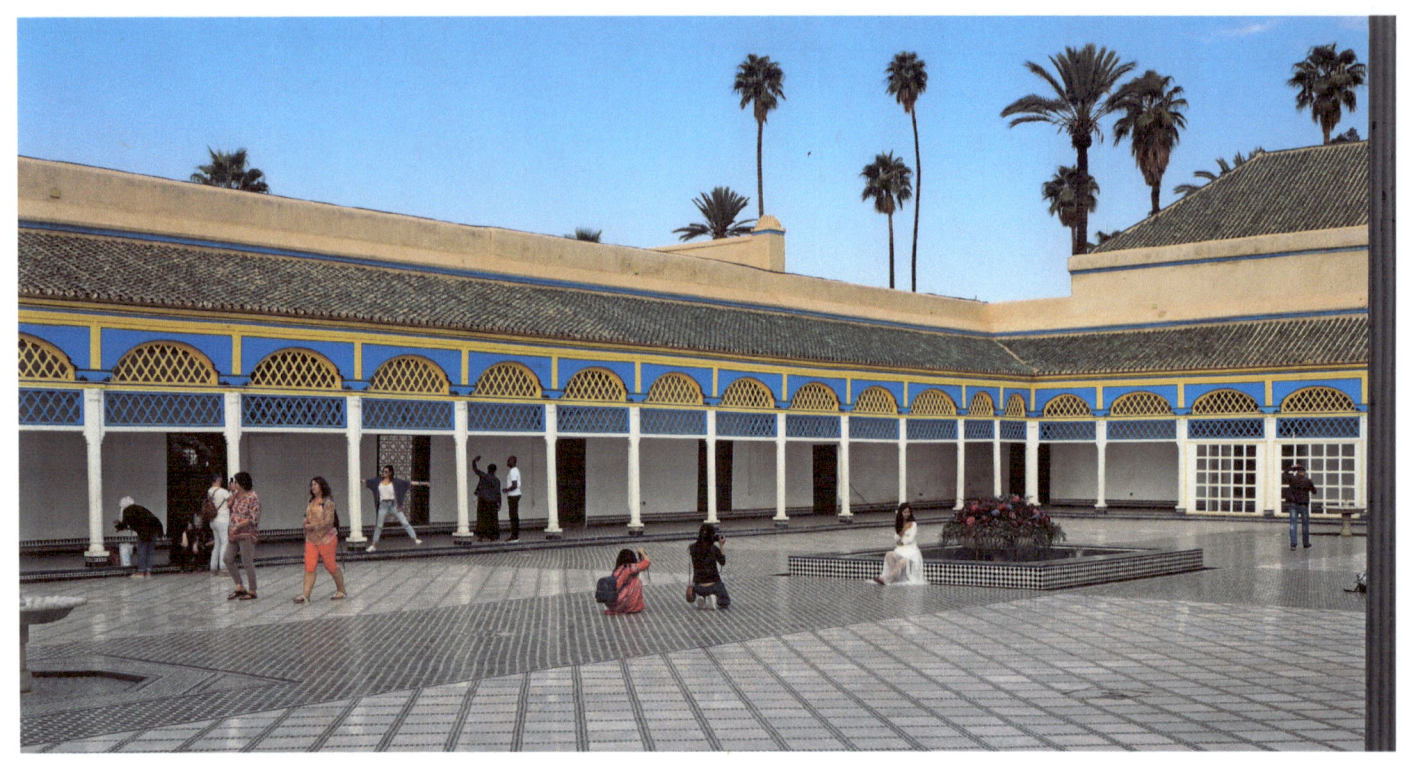

The Bahia Palace is a palace and a set of gardens located in Marrakesh, Morocco. It was built in the late 19th century, intended to be the greatest palace of its time. The name means "brilliance". As in other buildings of the period in other countries, it was intended to capture the essence of the Islamic and Moroccan style. There is a 2-acre (8,000 m²) garden with rooms opening onto courtyards.

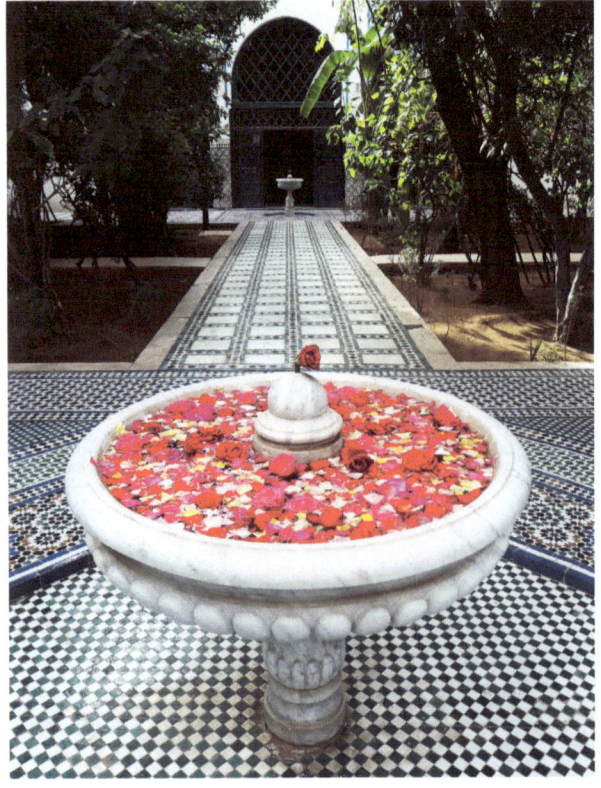

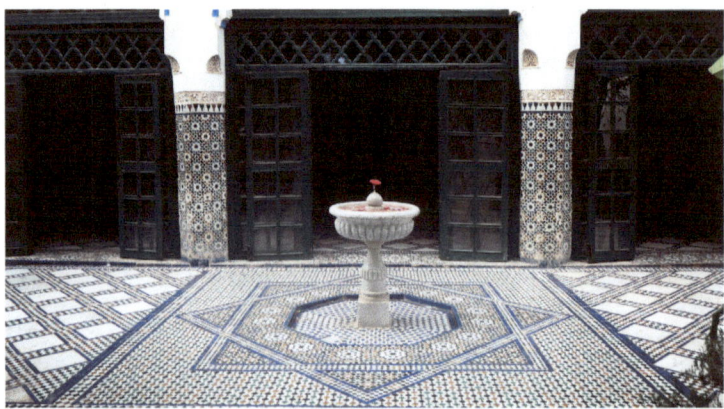

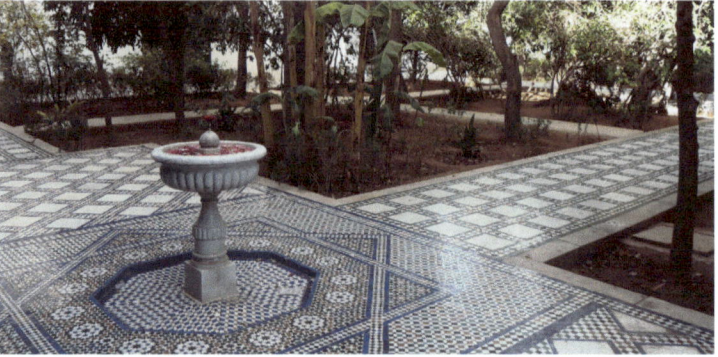

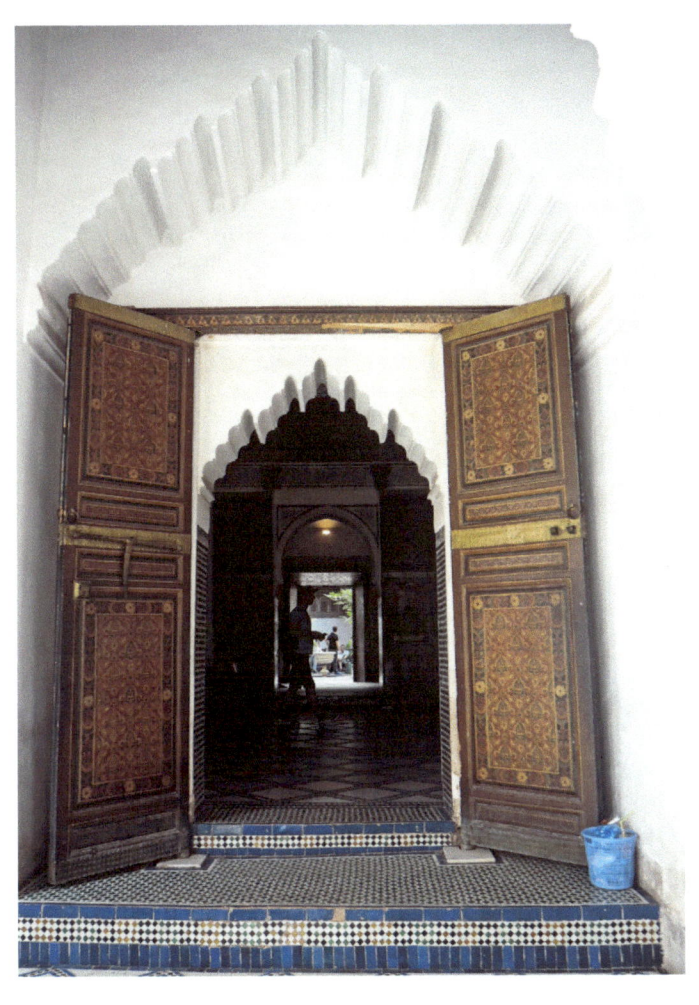
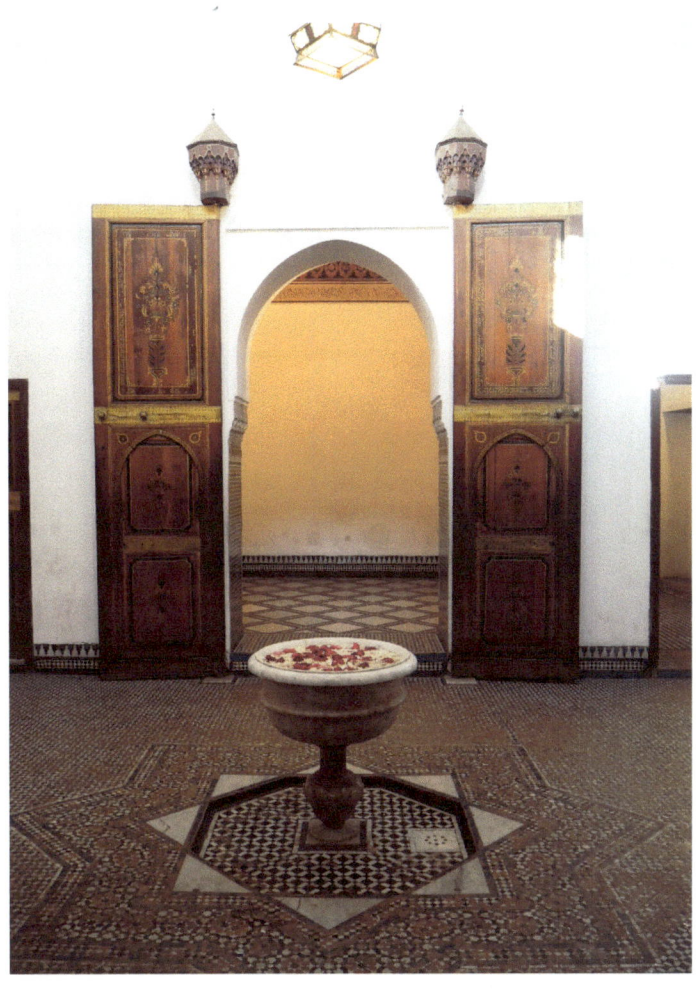
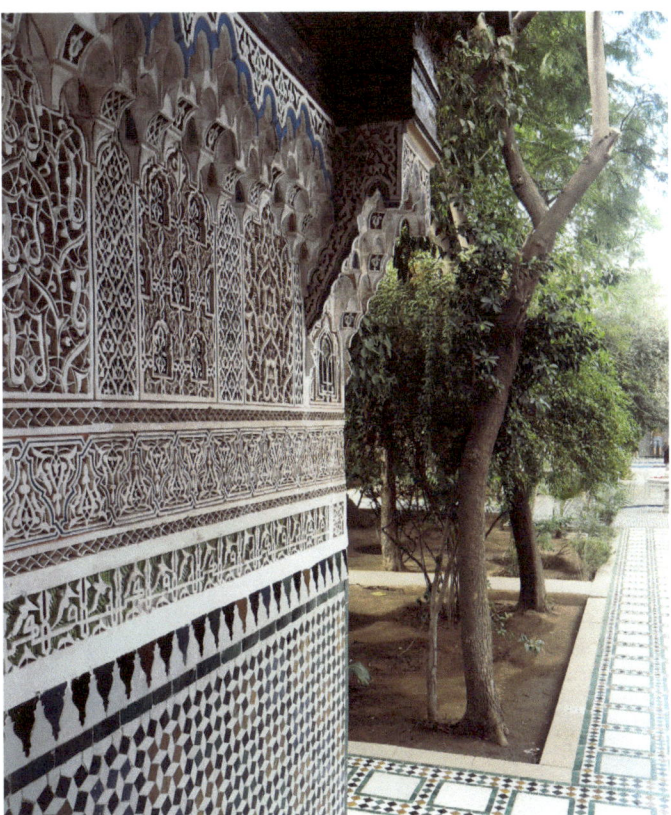
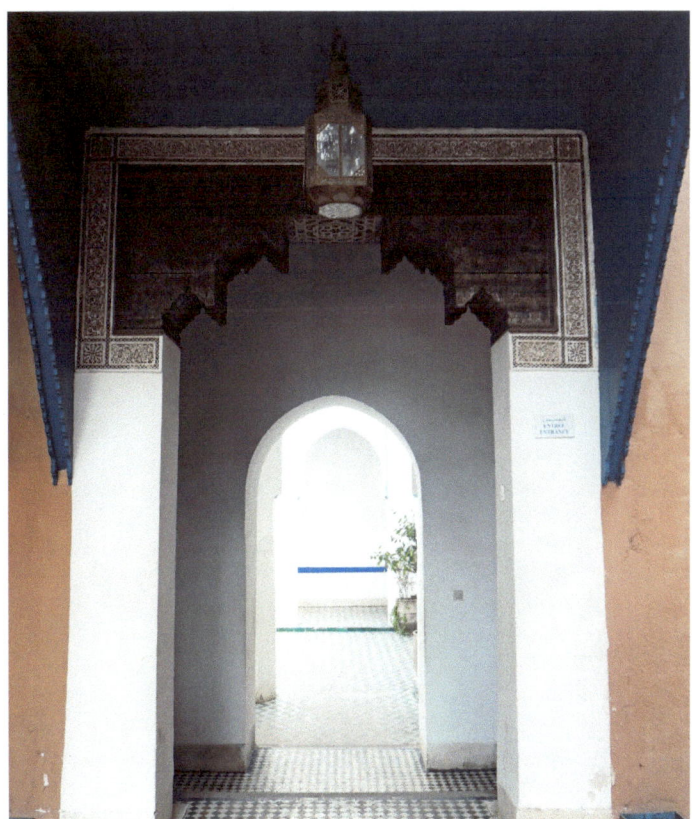

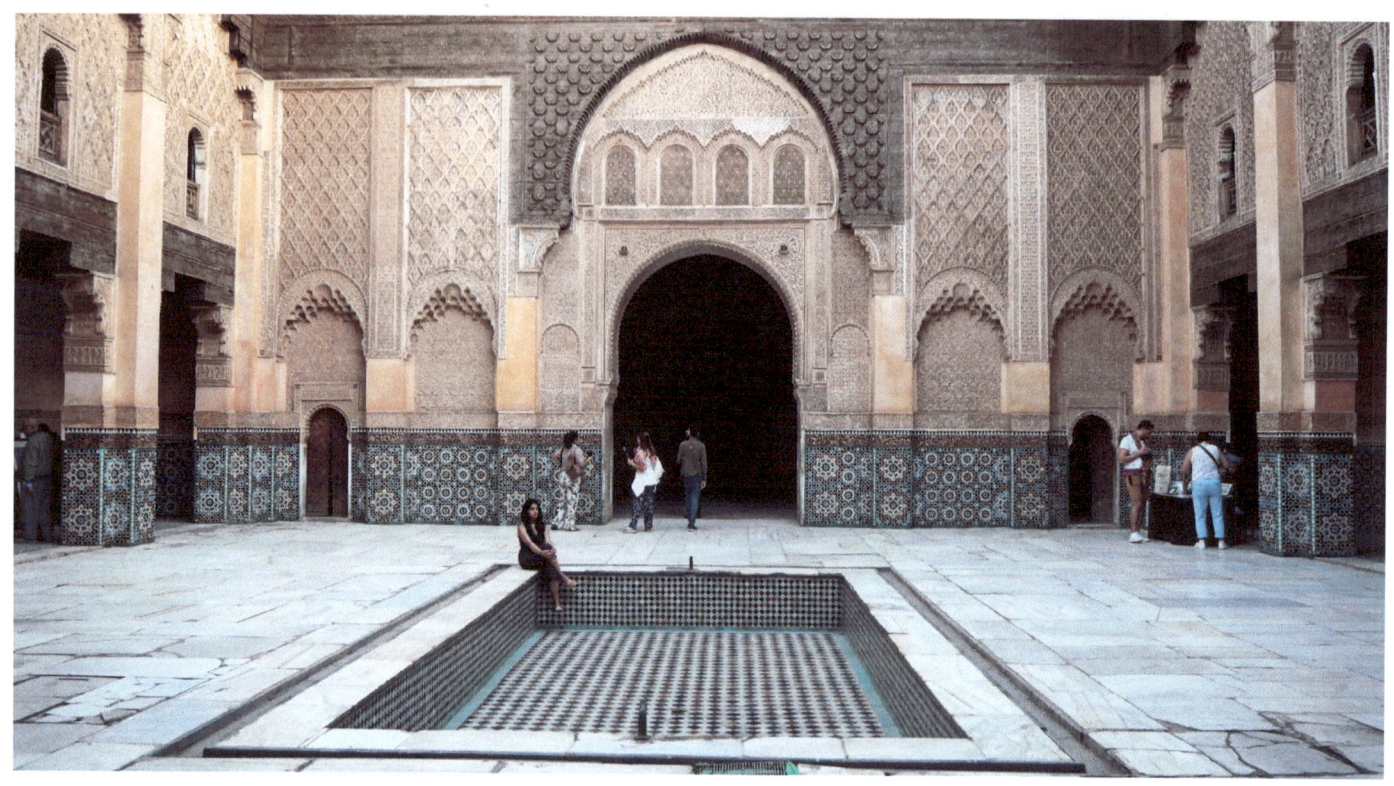

The Ben Youssef Madrasa is an Islamic college functioning today as an Islamic historical site, the Ben Youssef Madrasa was the largest Islamic college in Morocco during its height.

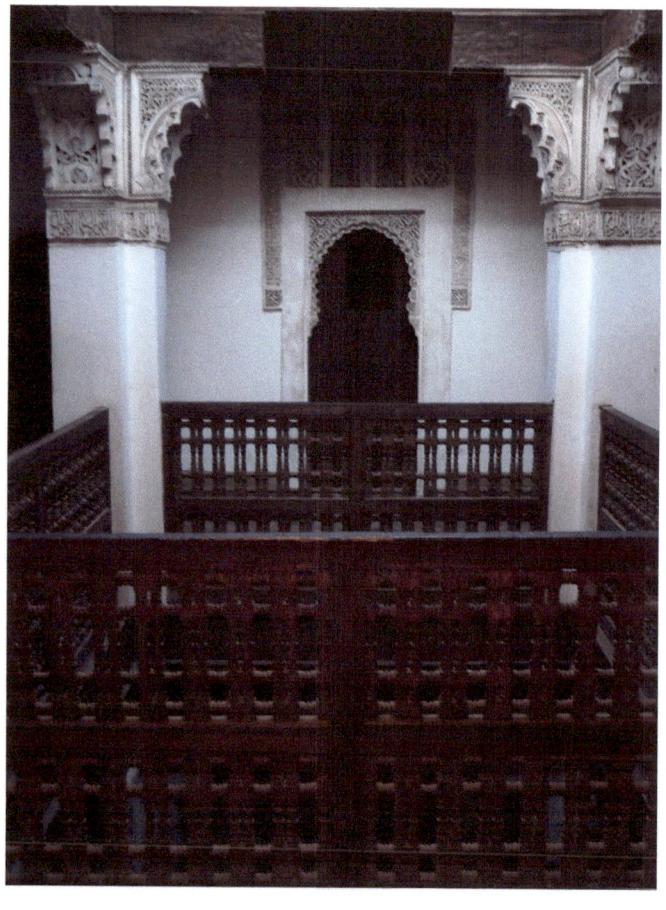

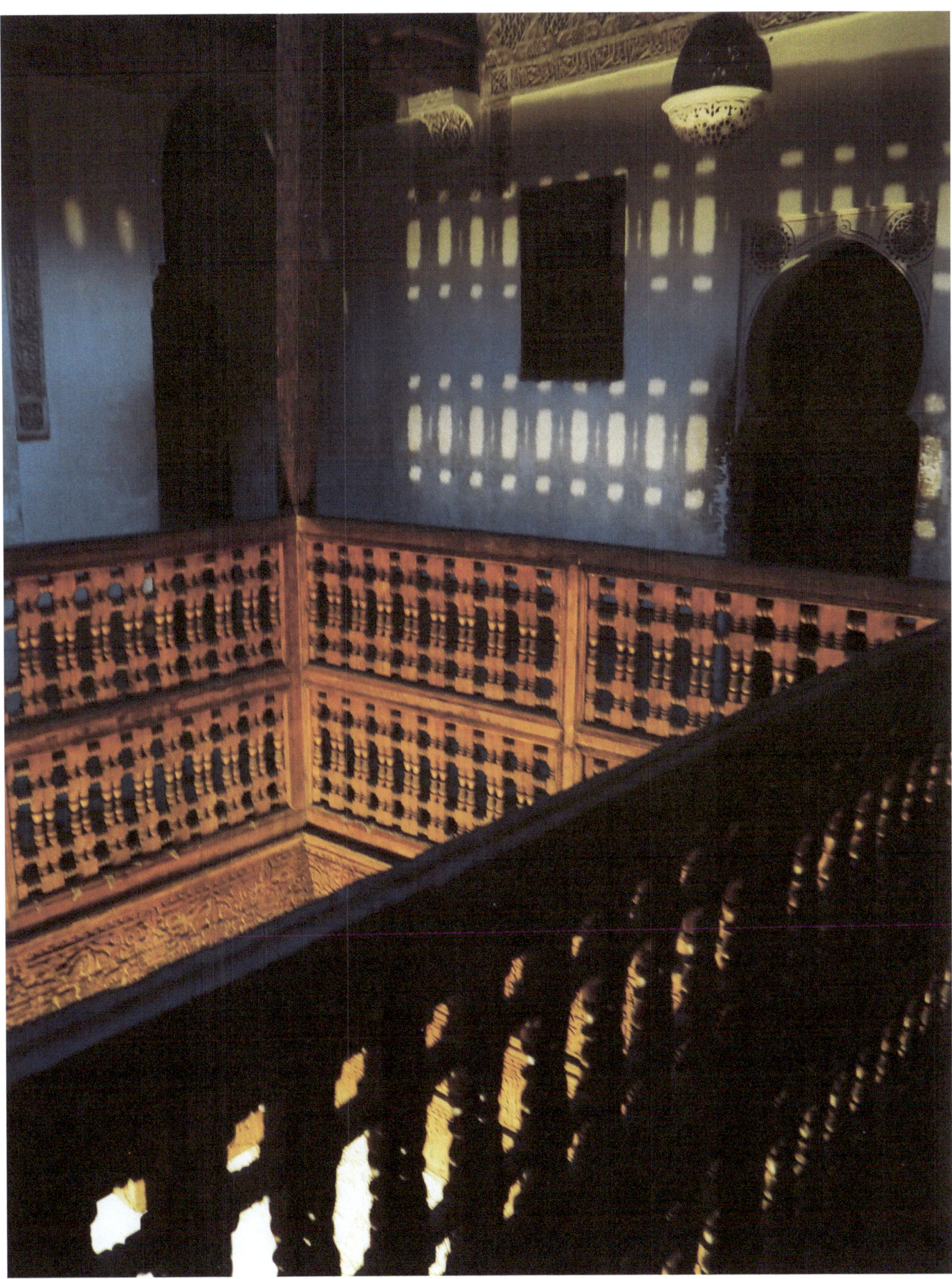

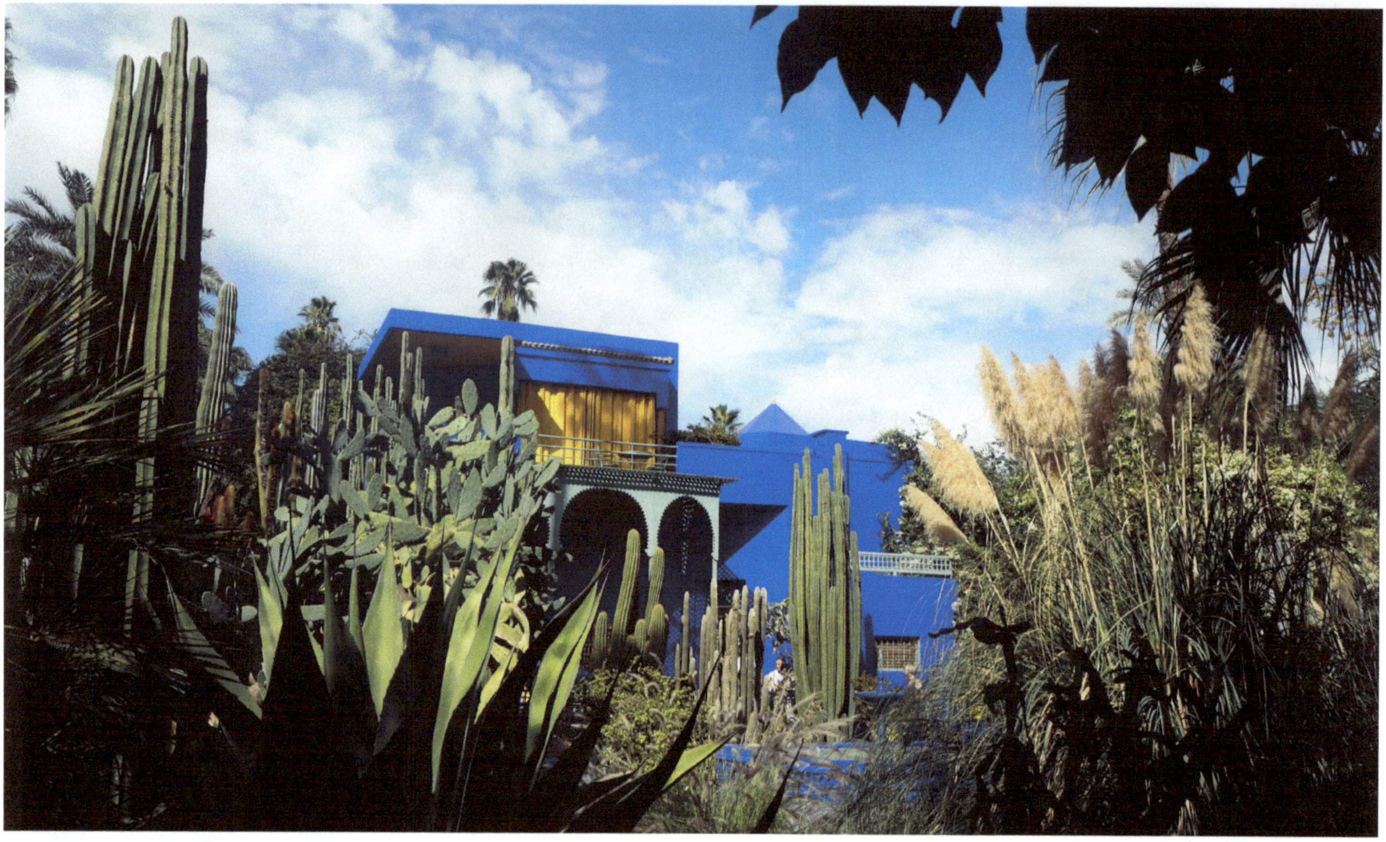

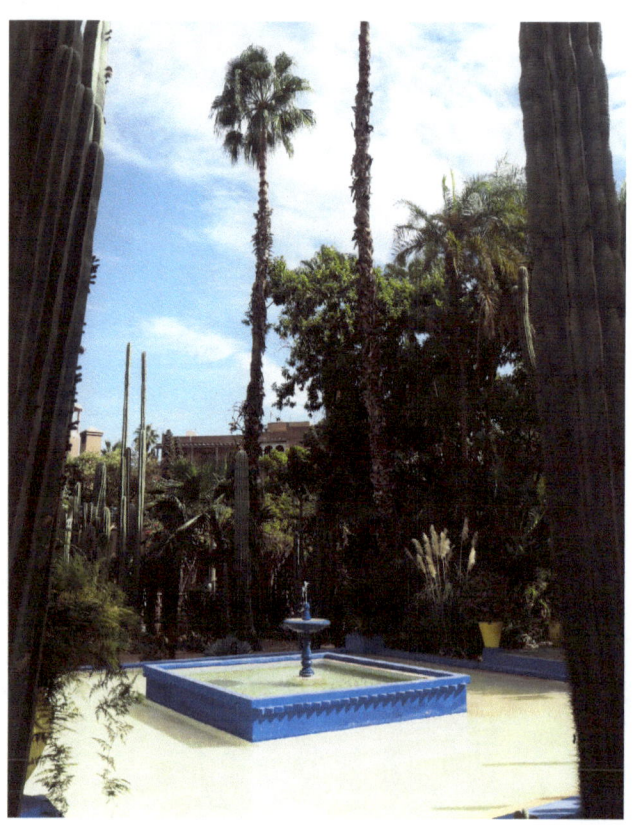

The Majorelle Garden is a botanical garden and artist's landscape garden, it was owned by Yves Saint-Laurent between 1980 and 2008. After Yves Saint Laurent died in 2008 his ashes were scattered in the Garden.

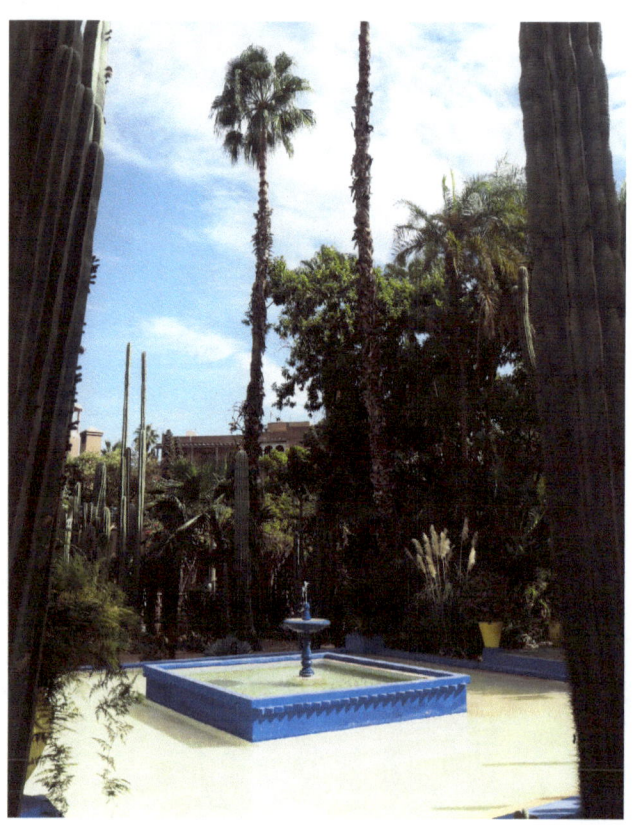
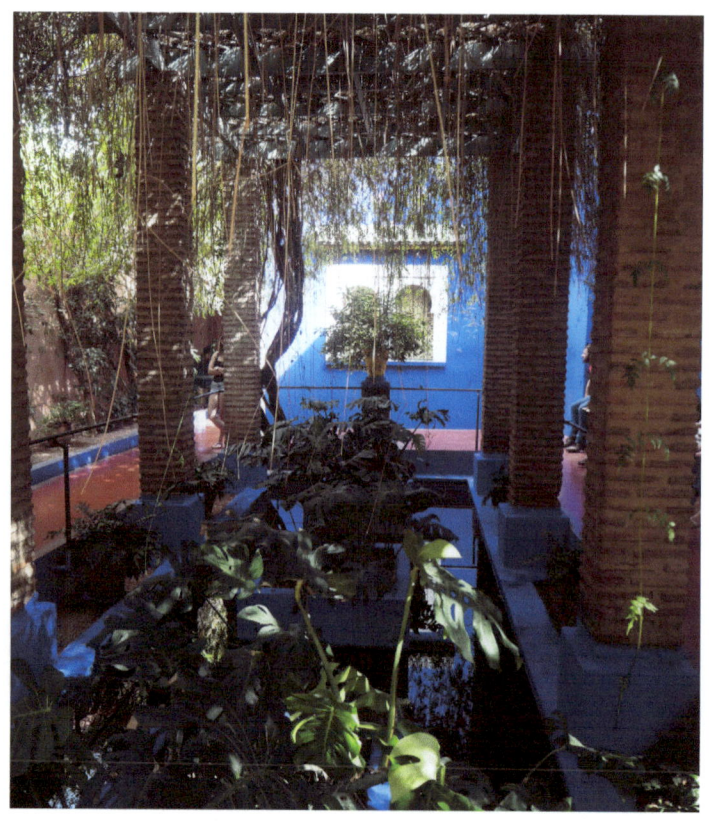

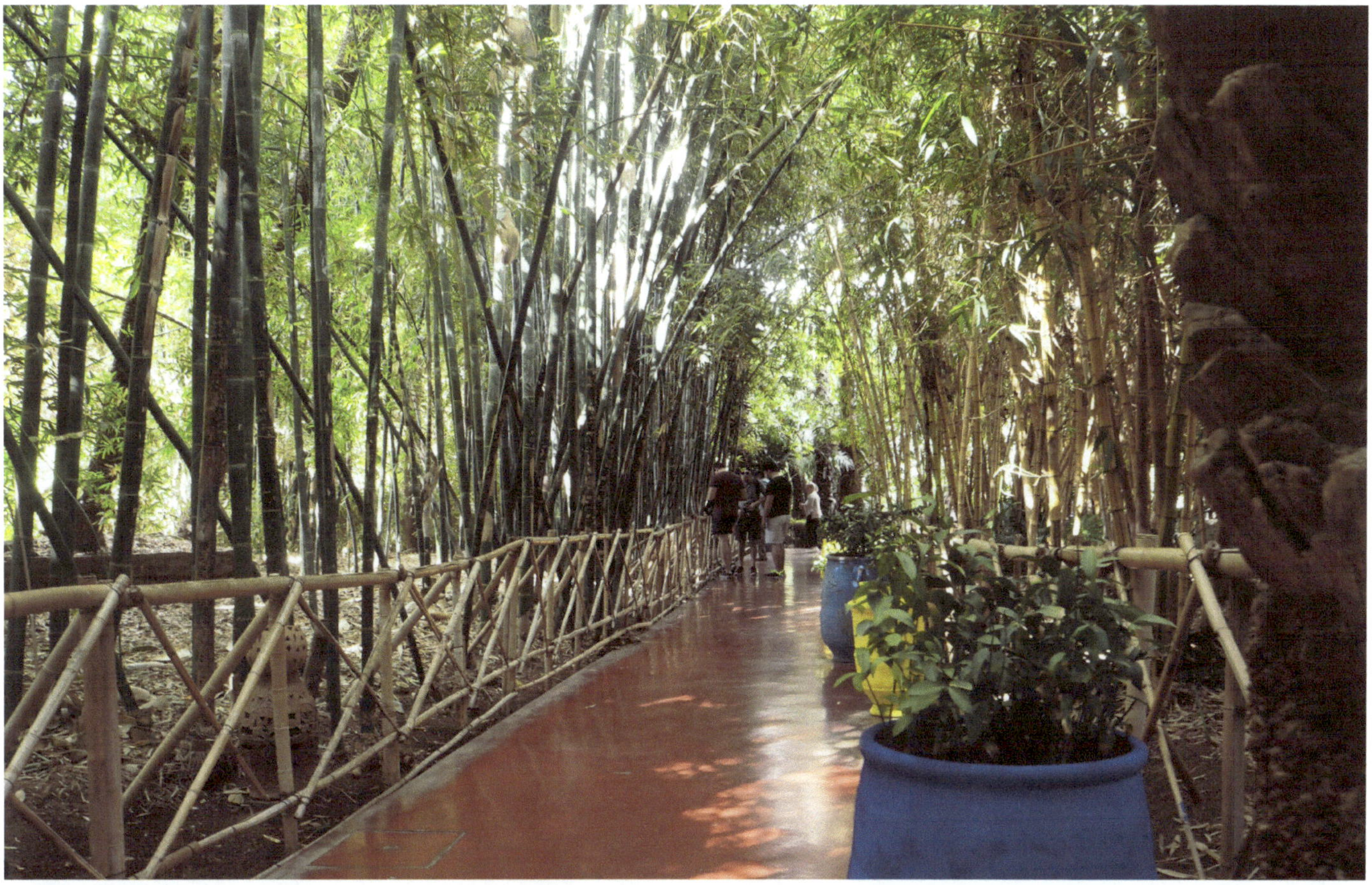

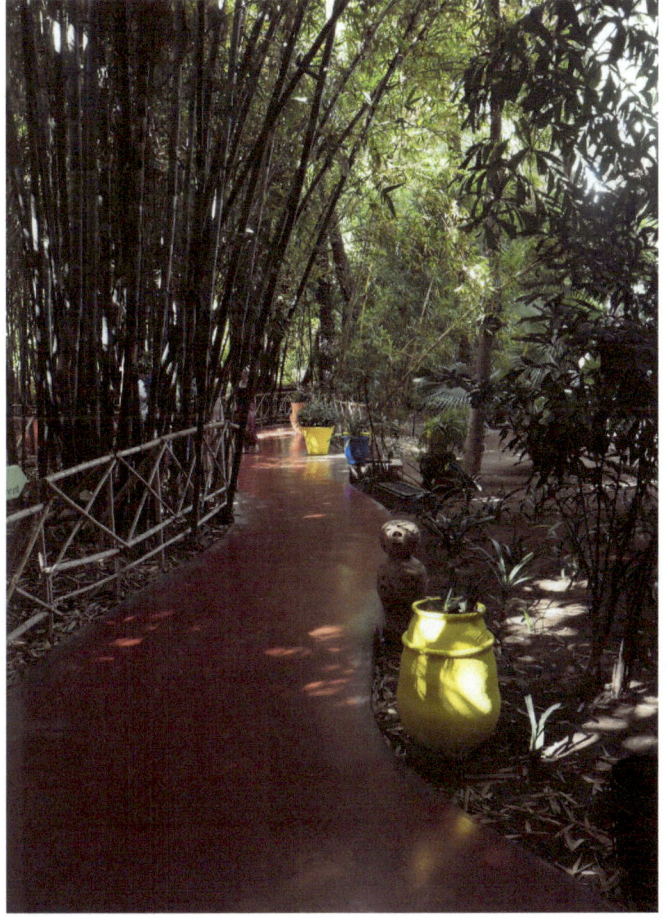

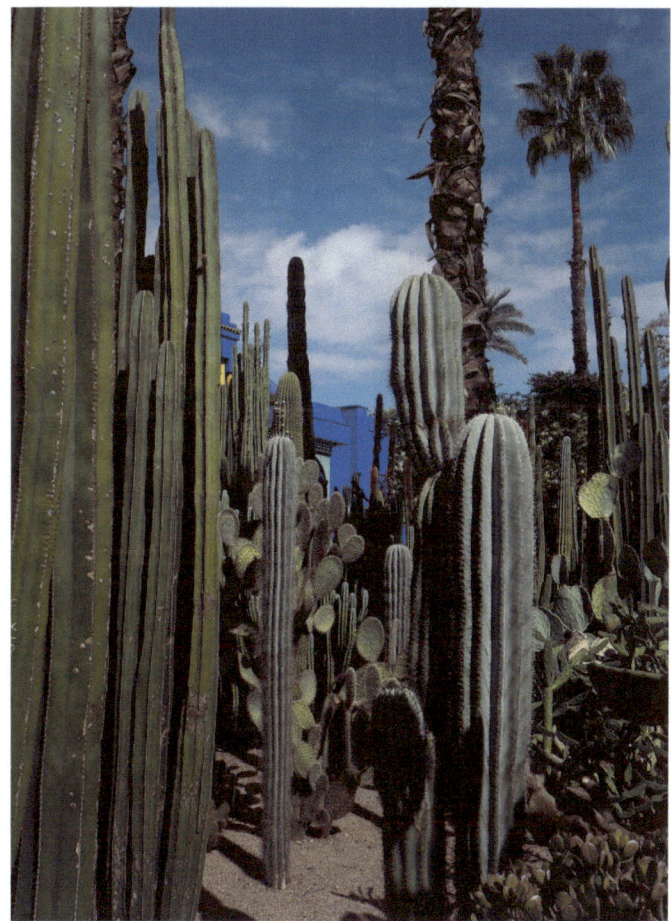

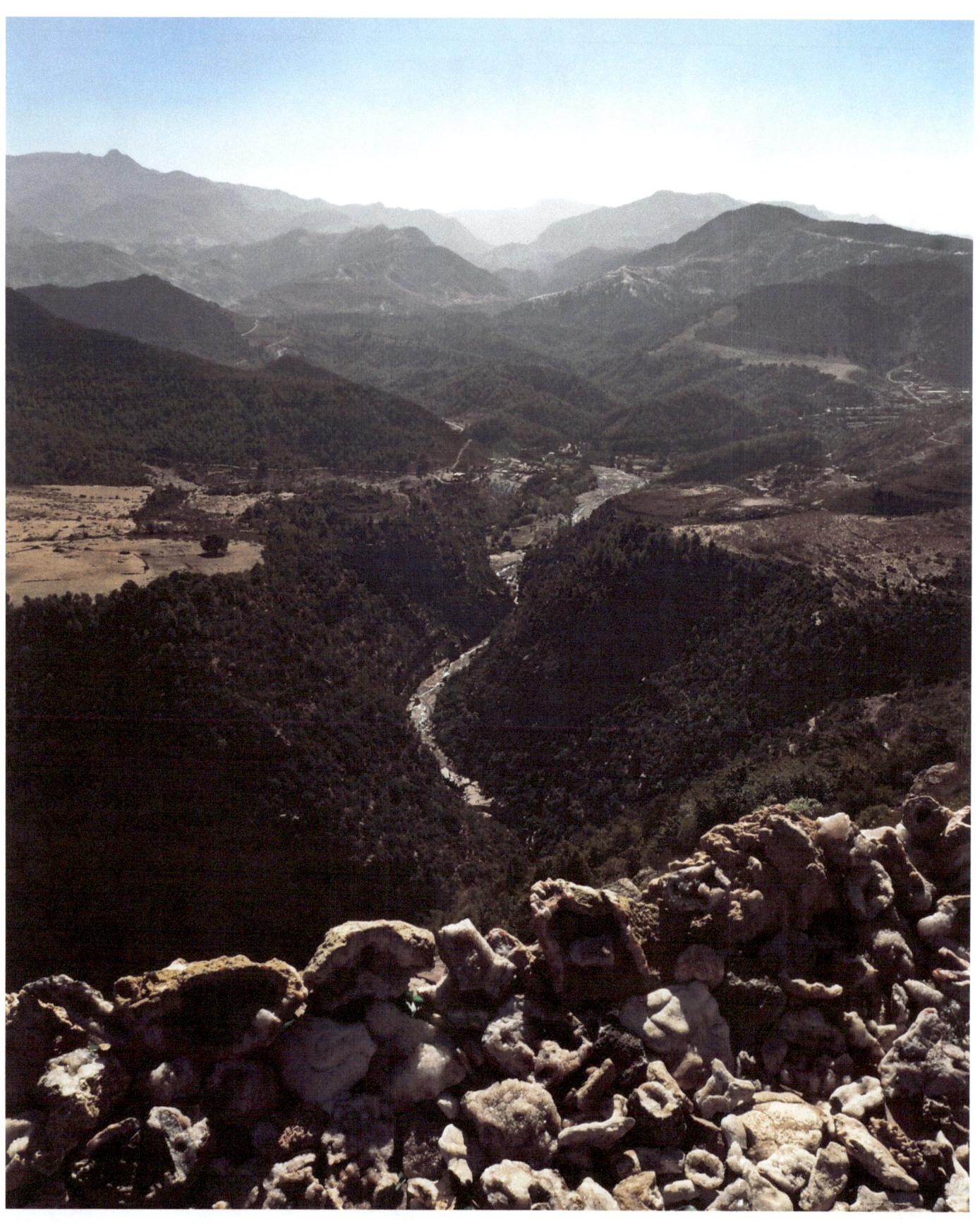

To reach the Sahara desert from the city of Marrakech you have to cross the Atlas mountain range.

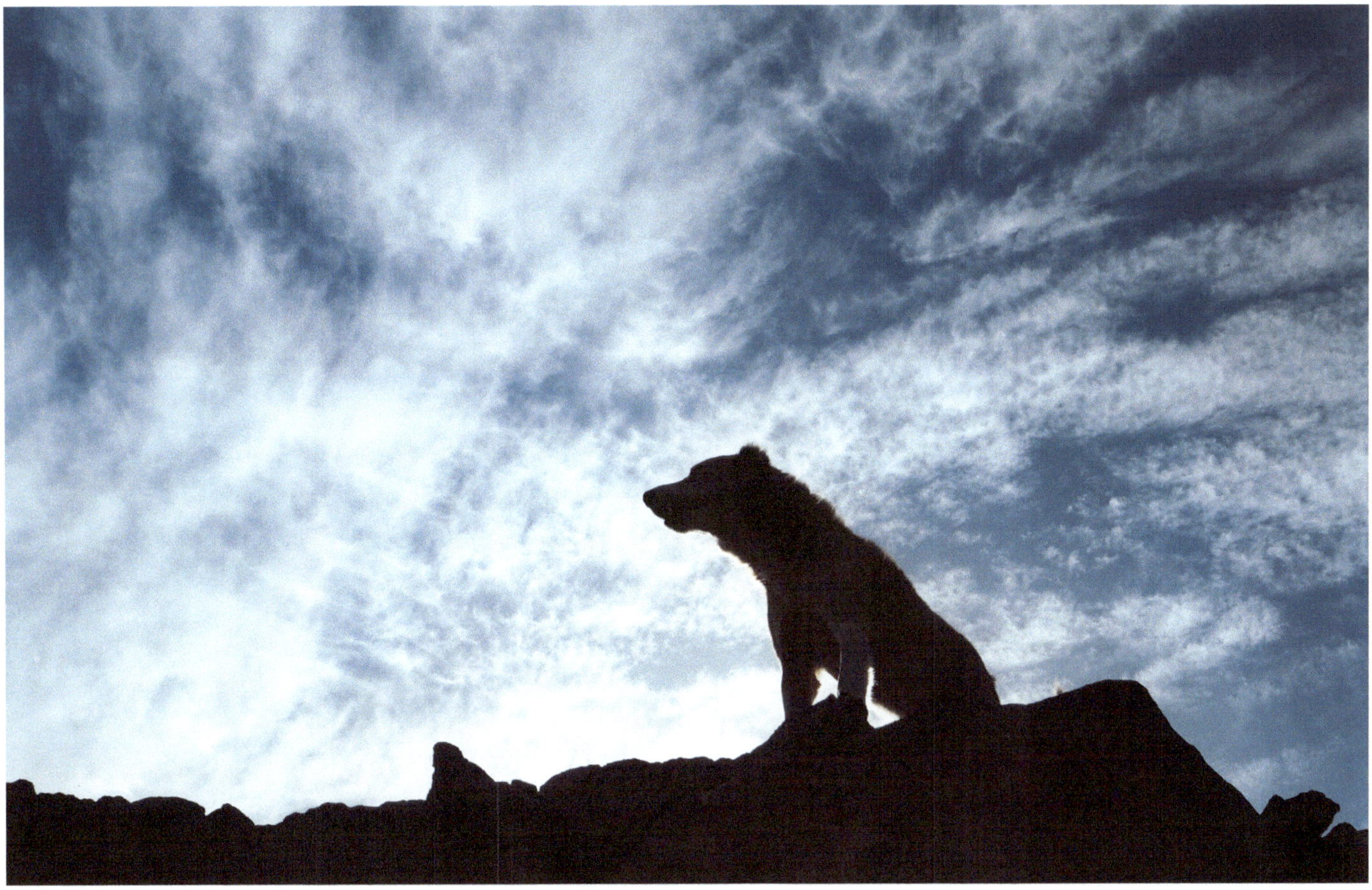

An amazing encounter with a mountains wild dog

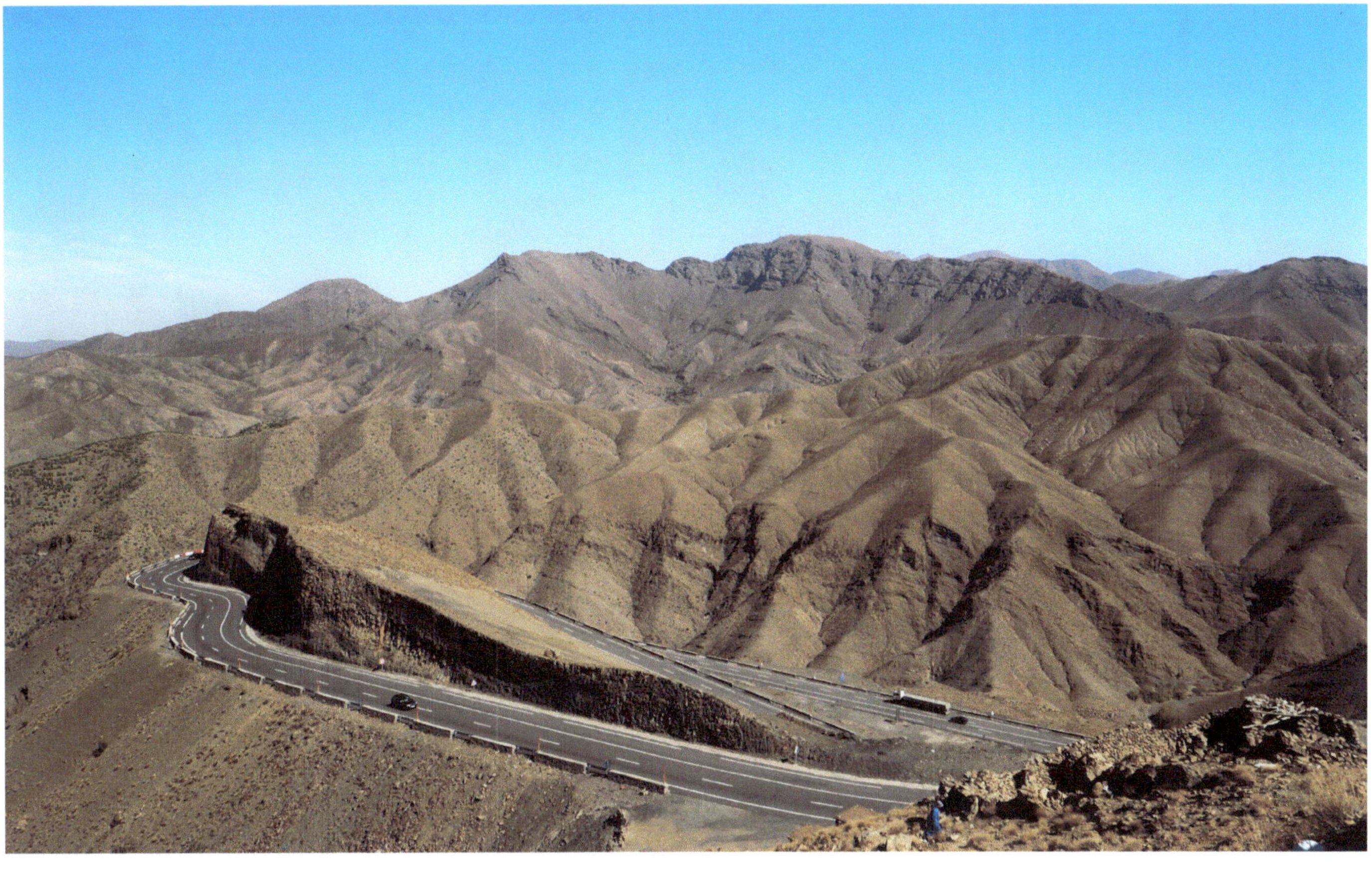

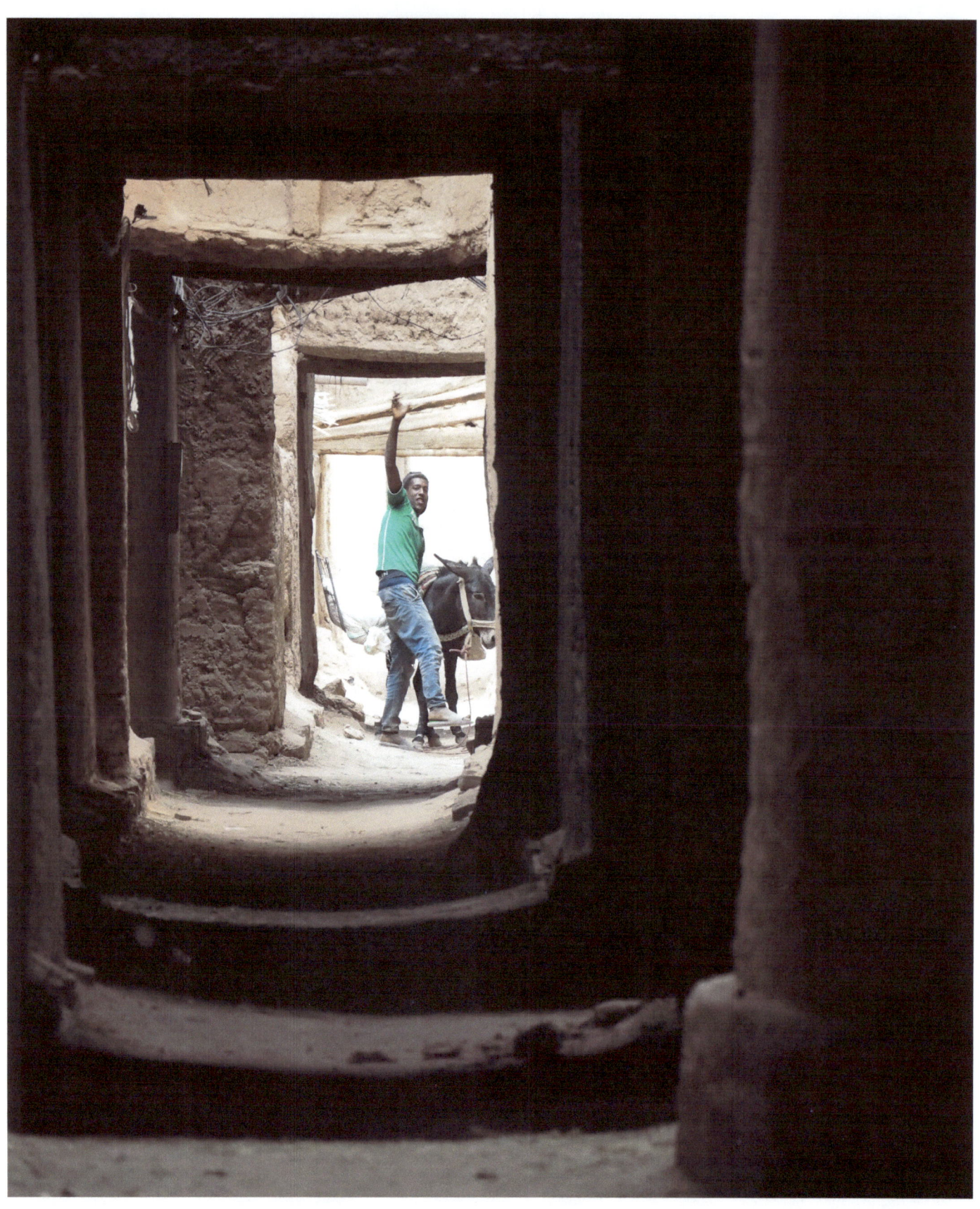

The populations of the villages we meet along the way prove to be very friendly and welcoming.

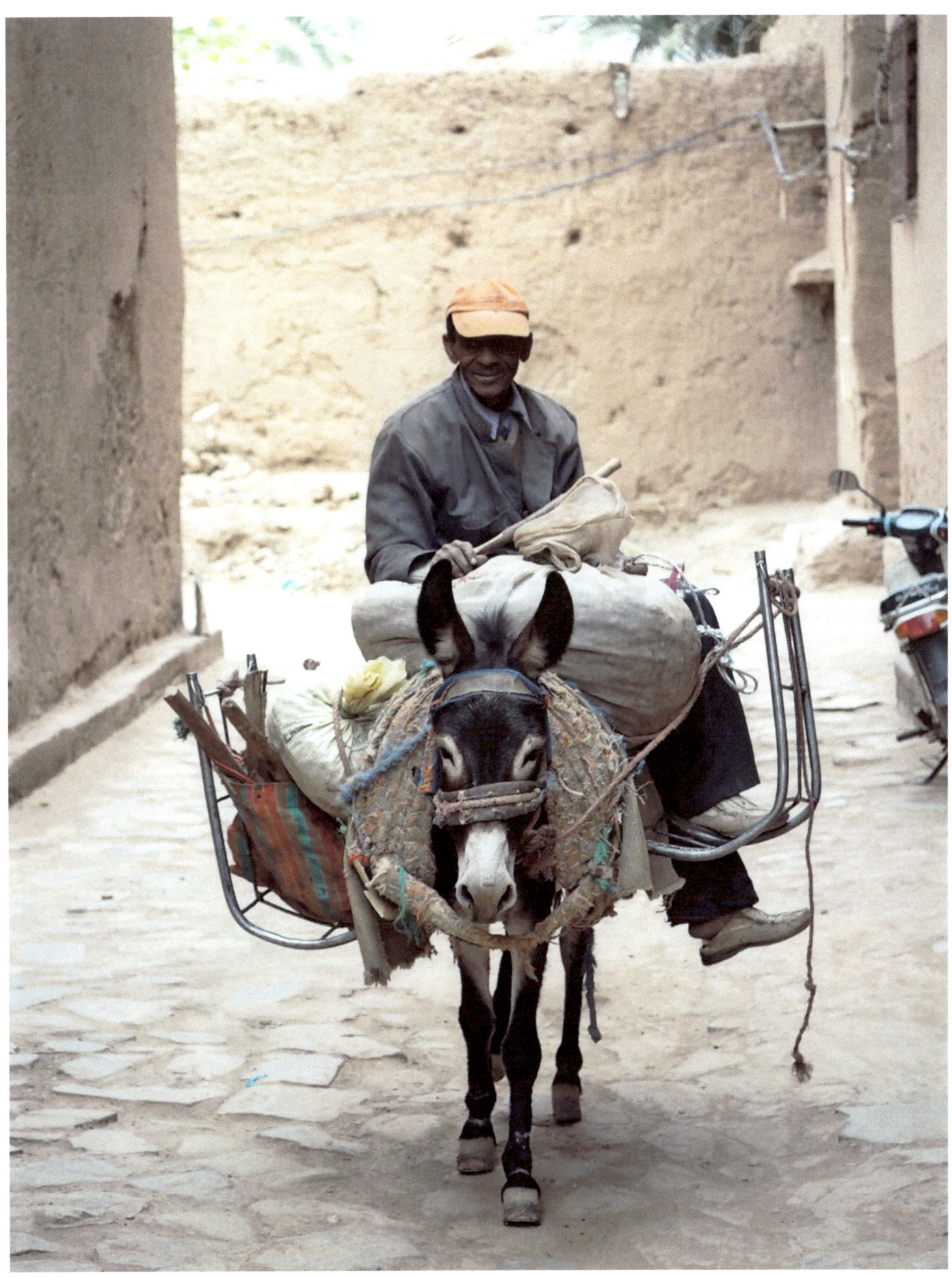

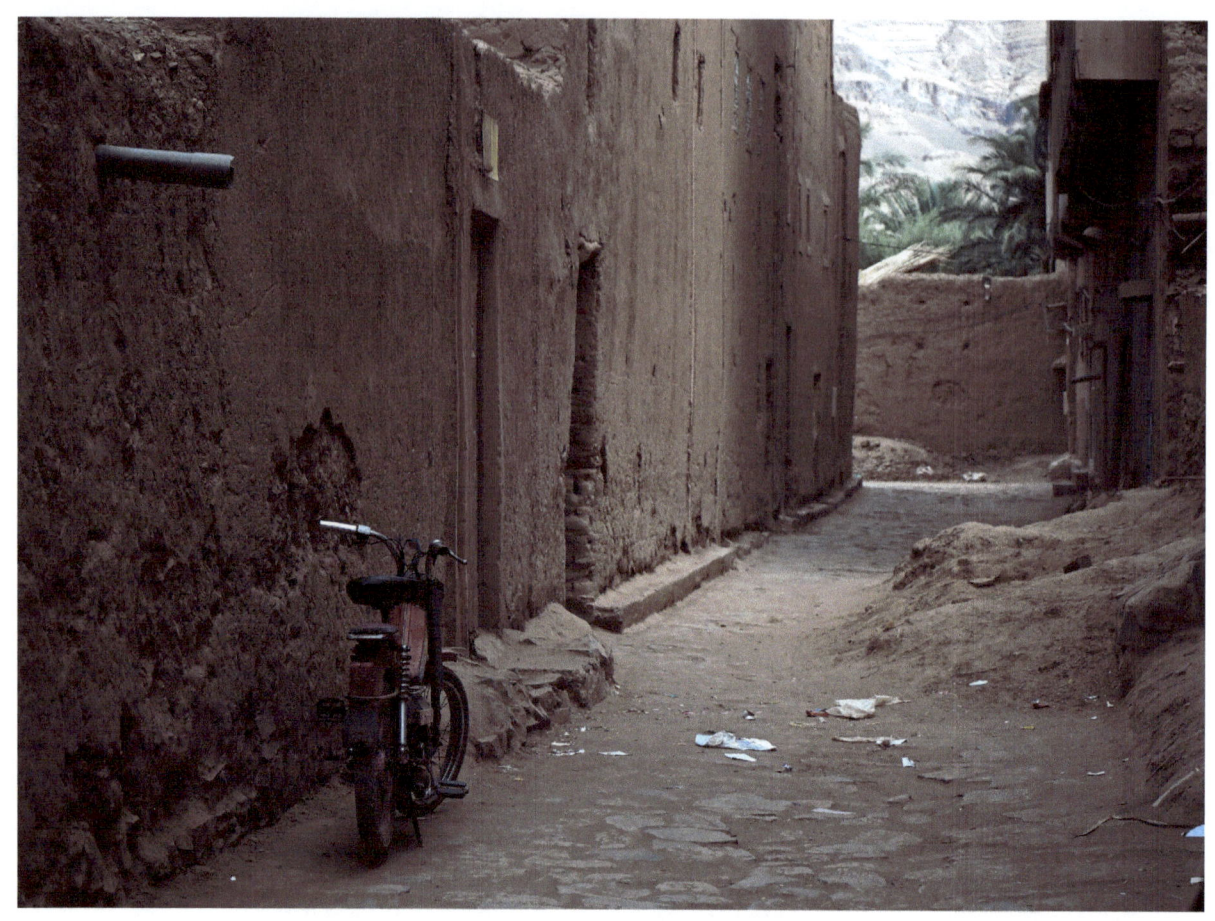

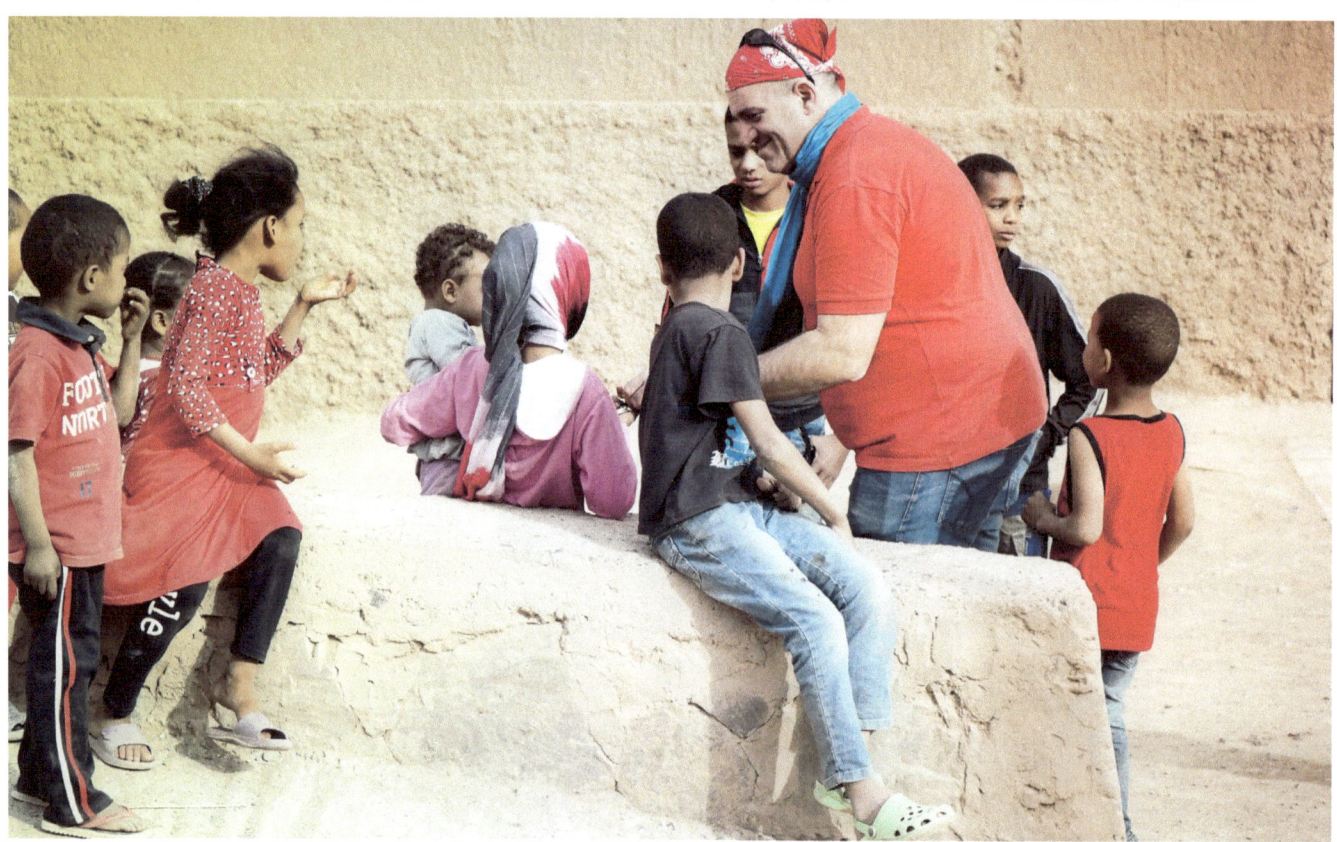

We brought some candies for the children of the village

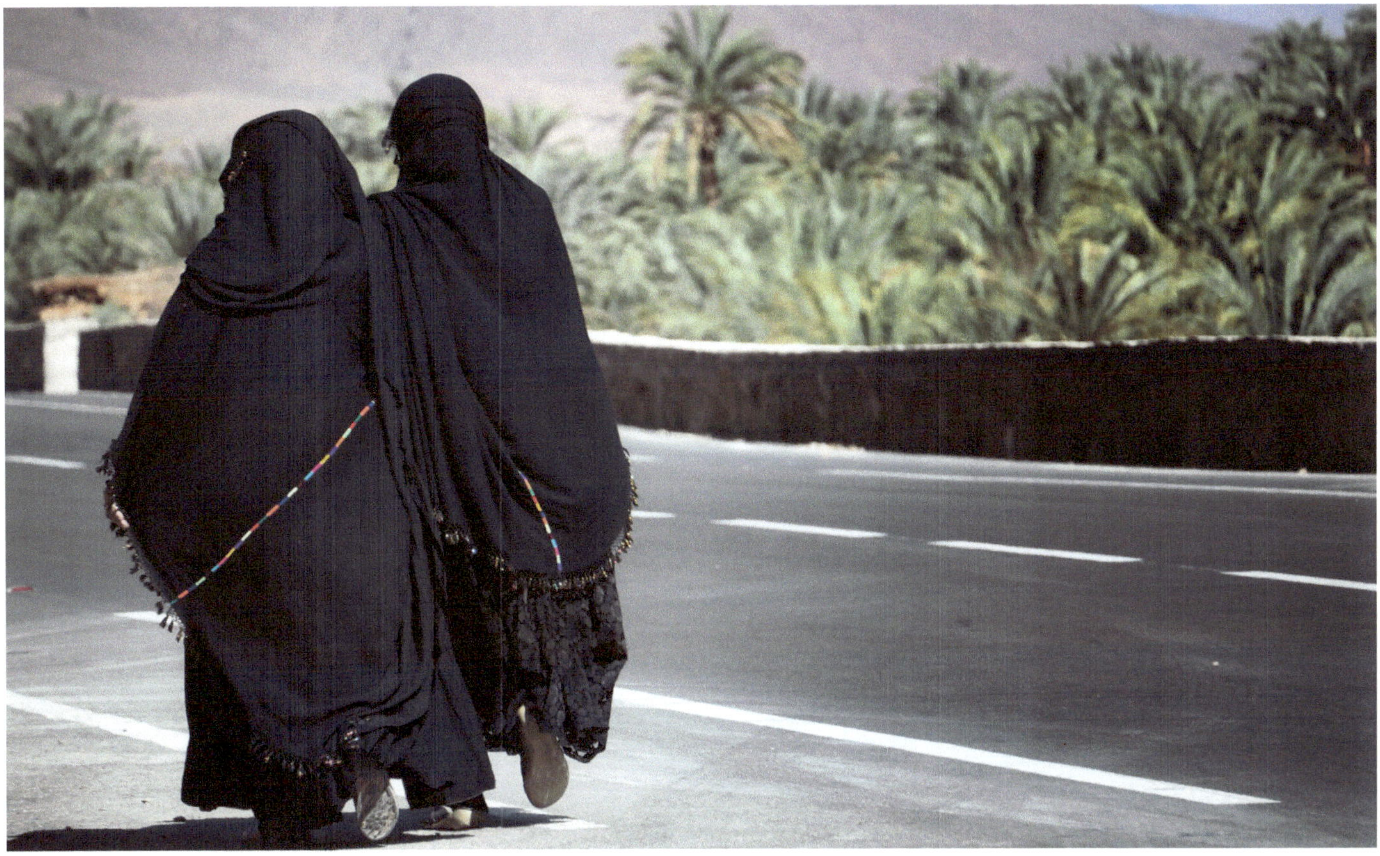

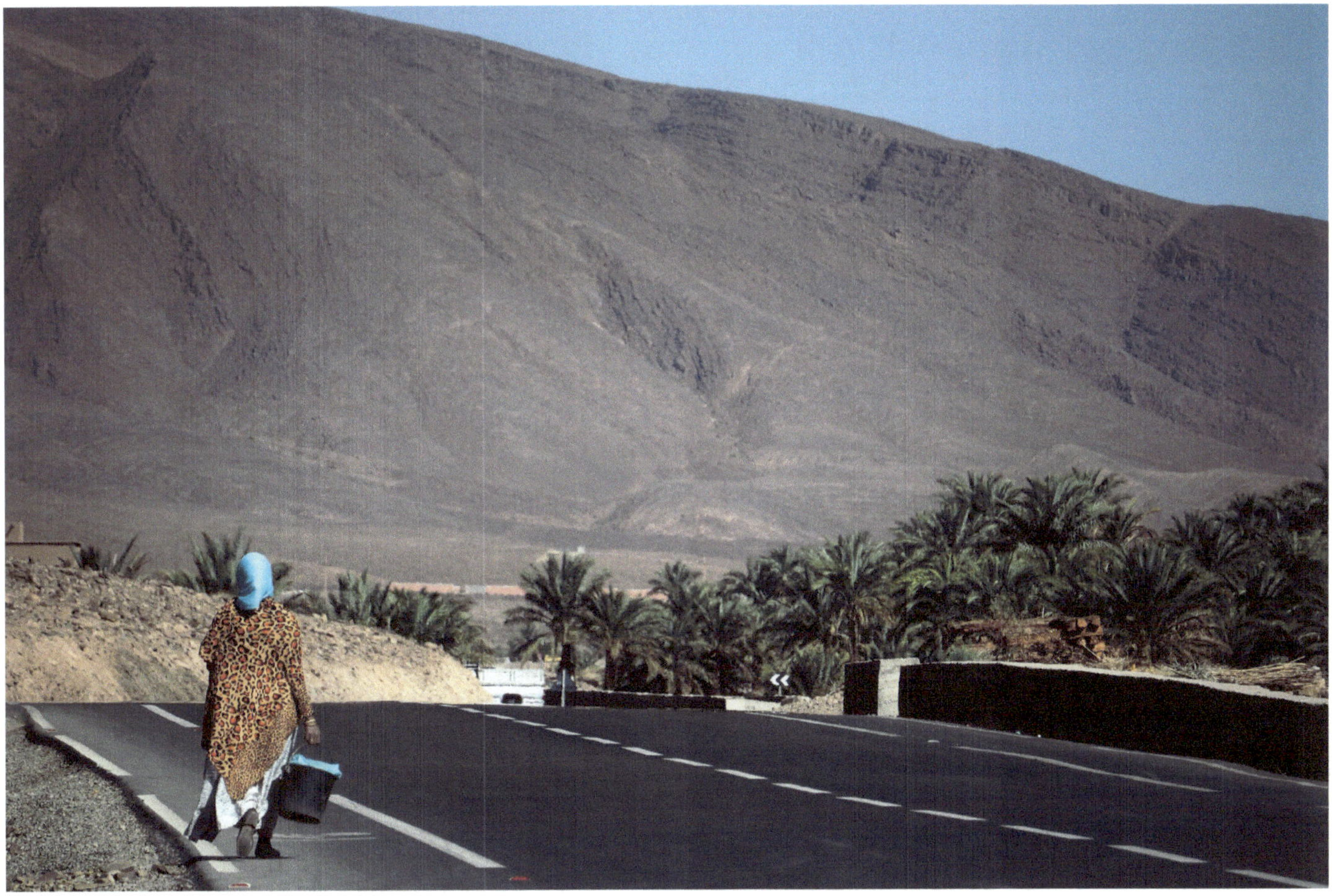

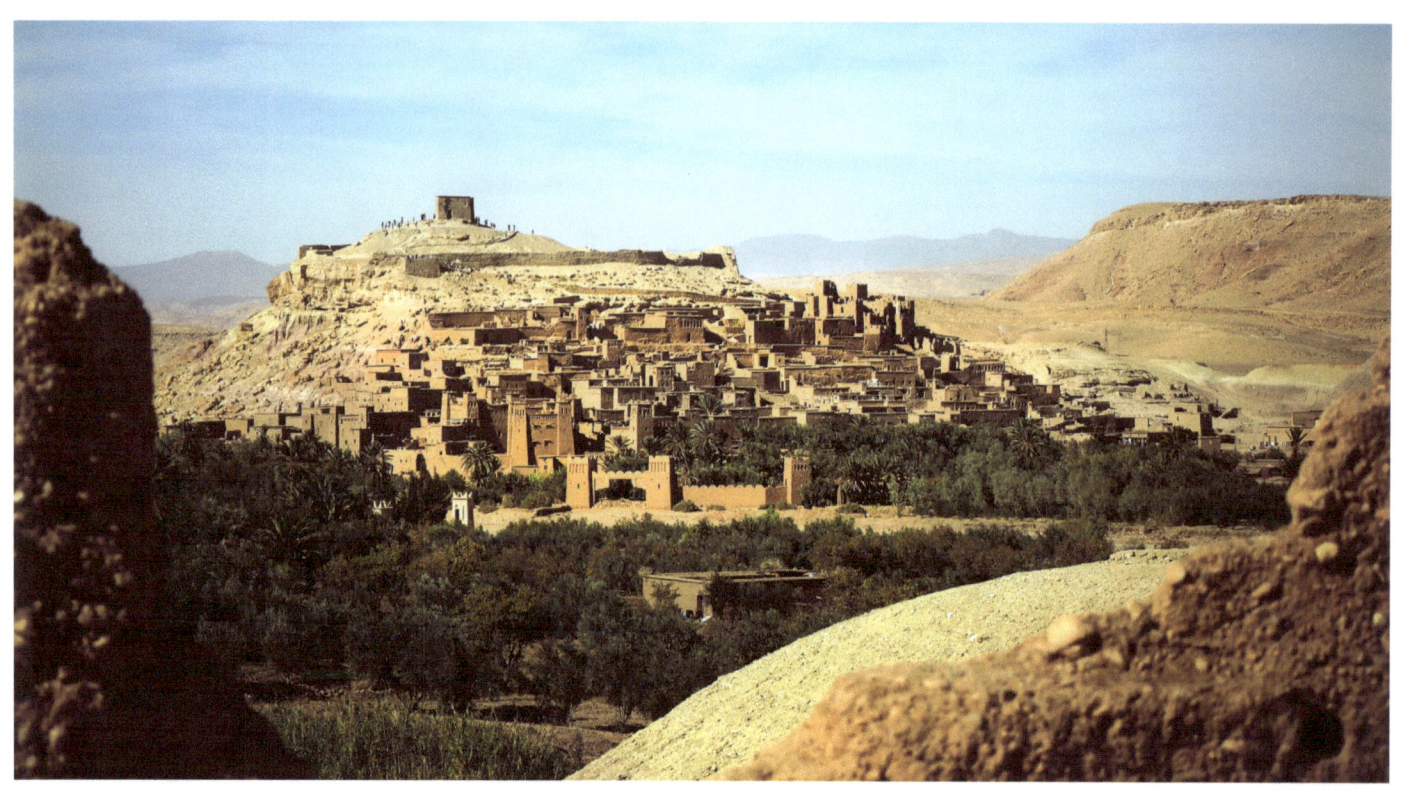

On the way to the great desert just past the Atlas mountain range we make a stop at the fortified city of **Aït Benhaddou,** an ighrem (fortified village in English) (ksar in Arabic), along the former caravan route between the Sahara and Marrakech in present-day Morocco. Inside the walls of the ksar are half a dozen kasbahs, or merchants' houses. Ksar Aït Benhaddou is a great example of Moroccan earthen clay architecture and has been a UNESCO World Heritage Site since 1987. To discover the wonders of the city, we hire a local Berber guide.

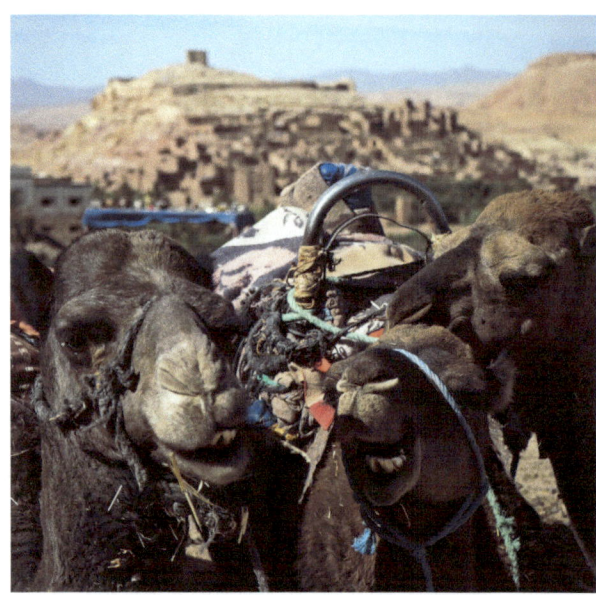

camel photobombers

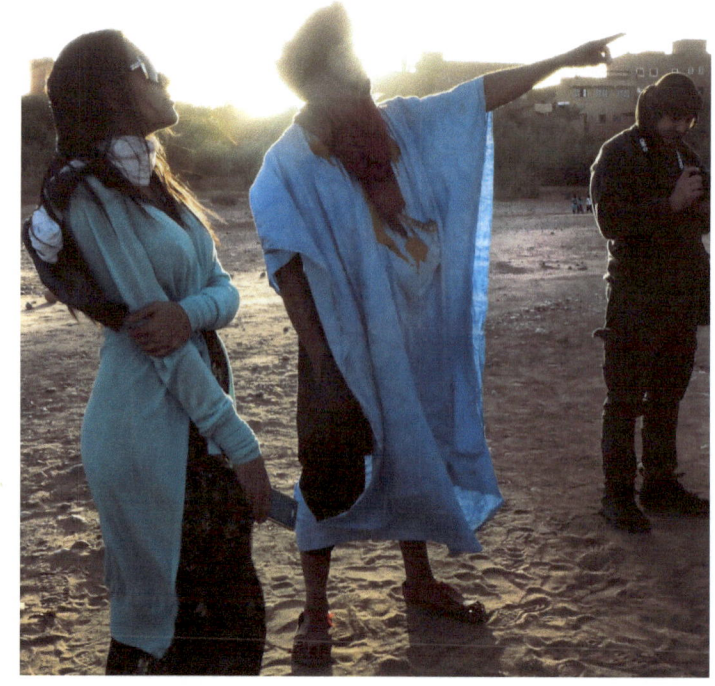

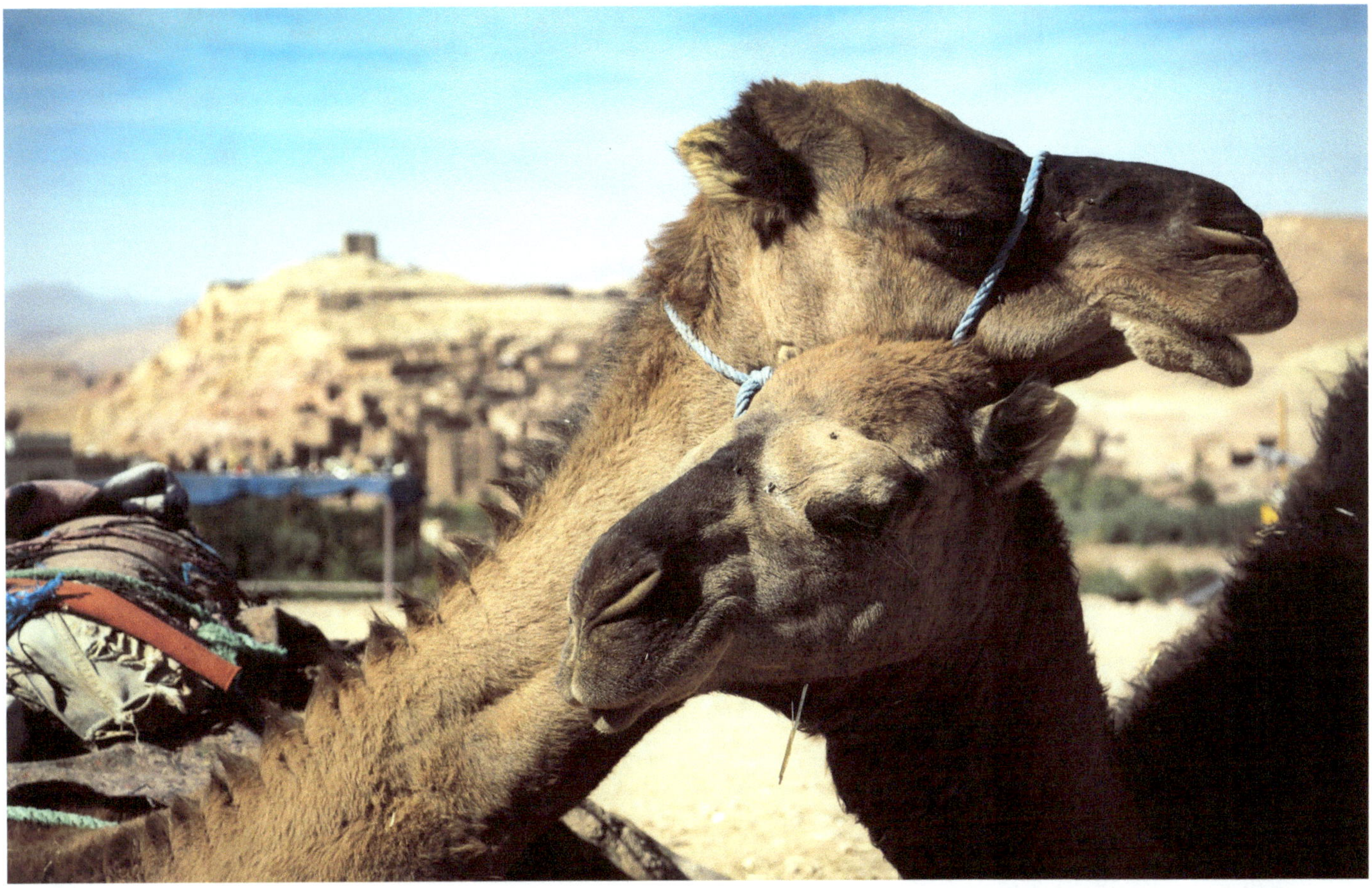

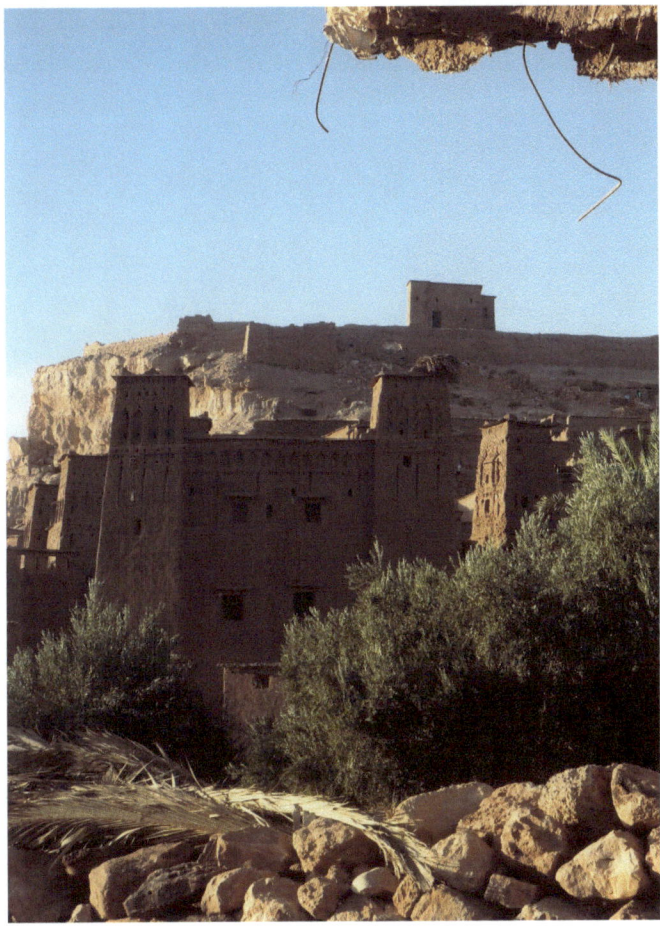

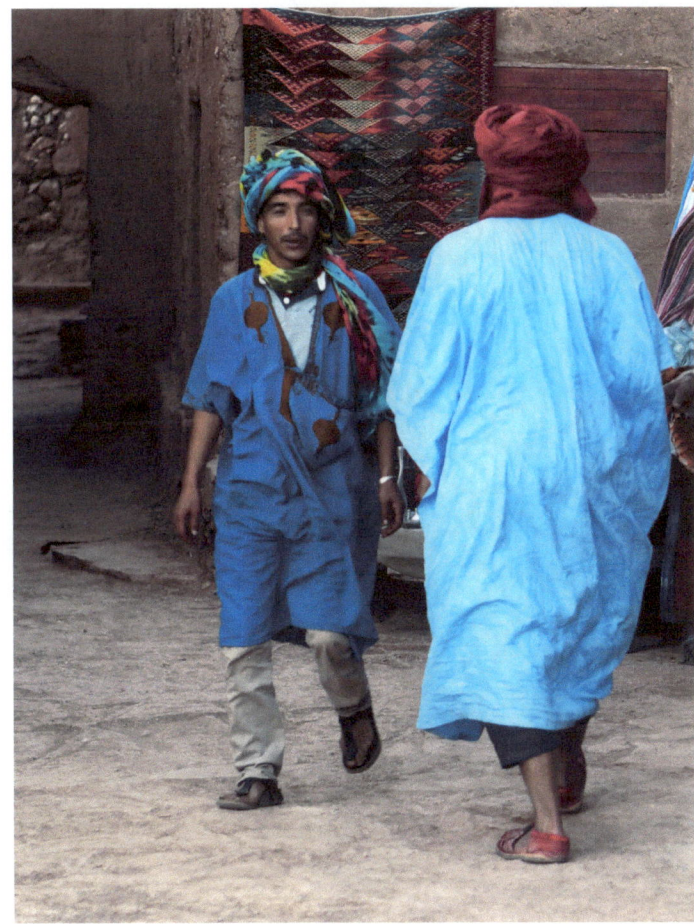

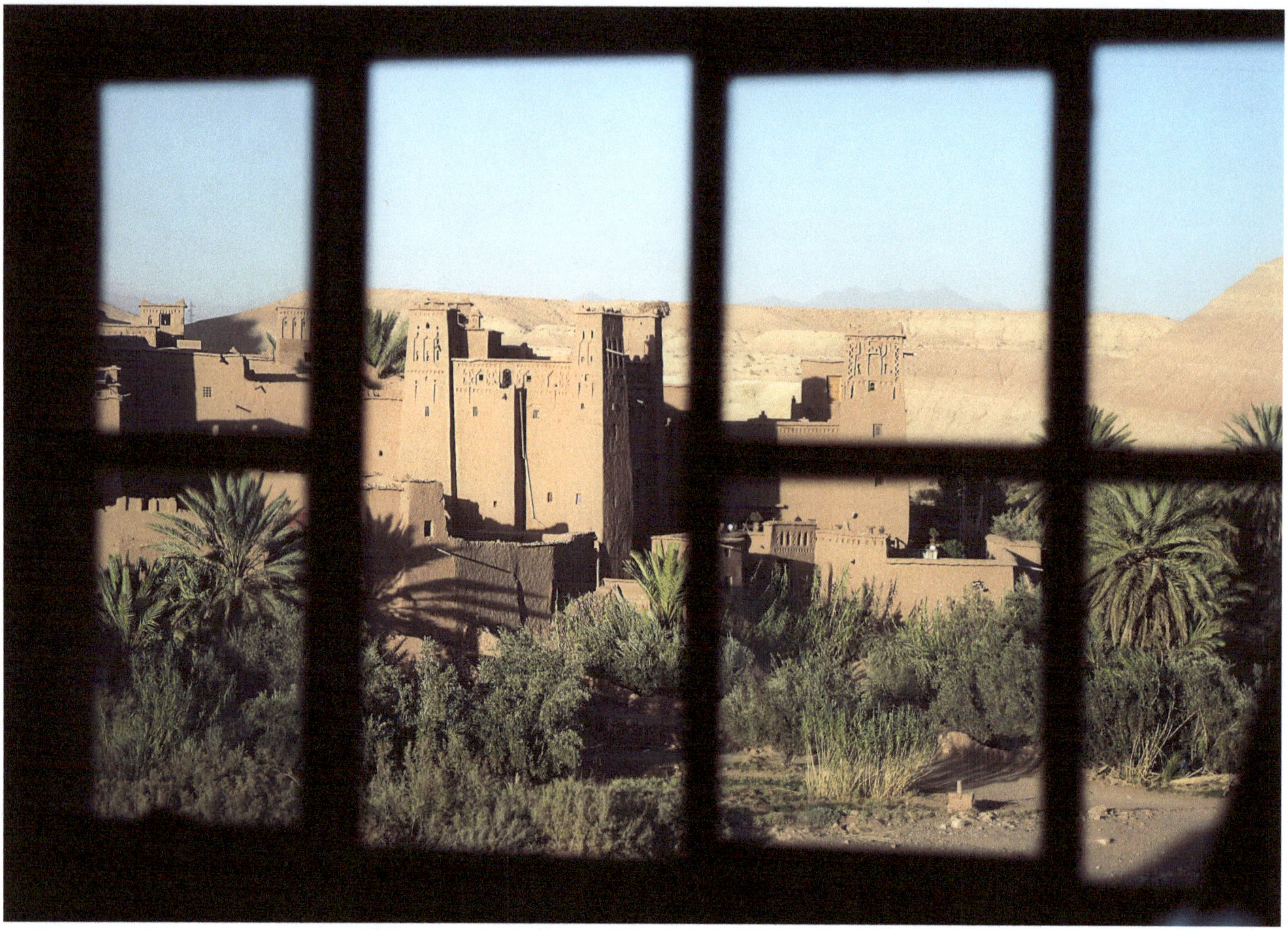

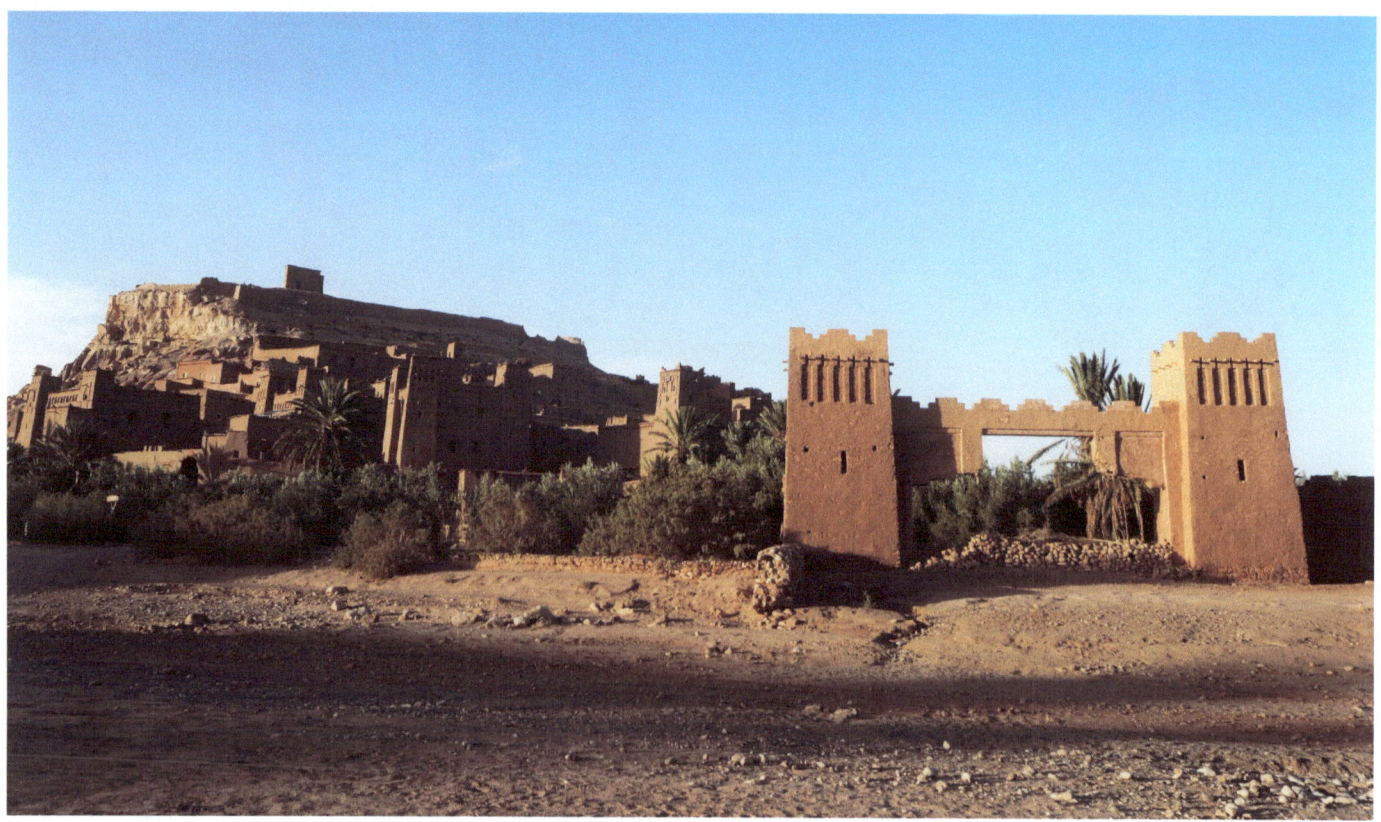

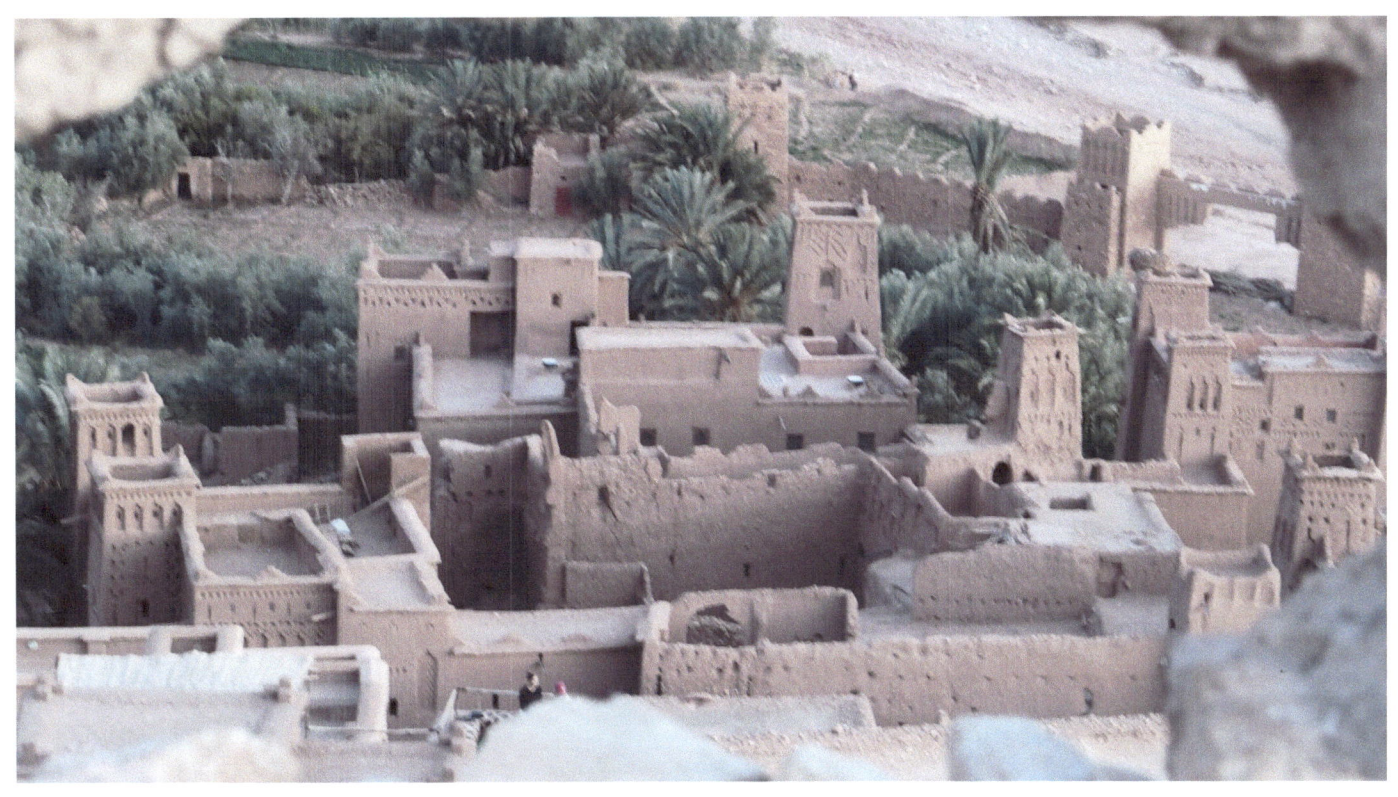

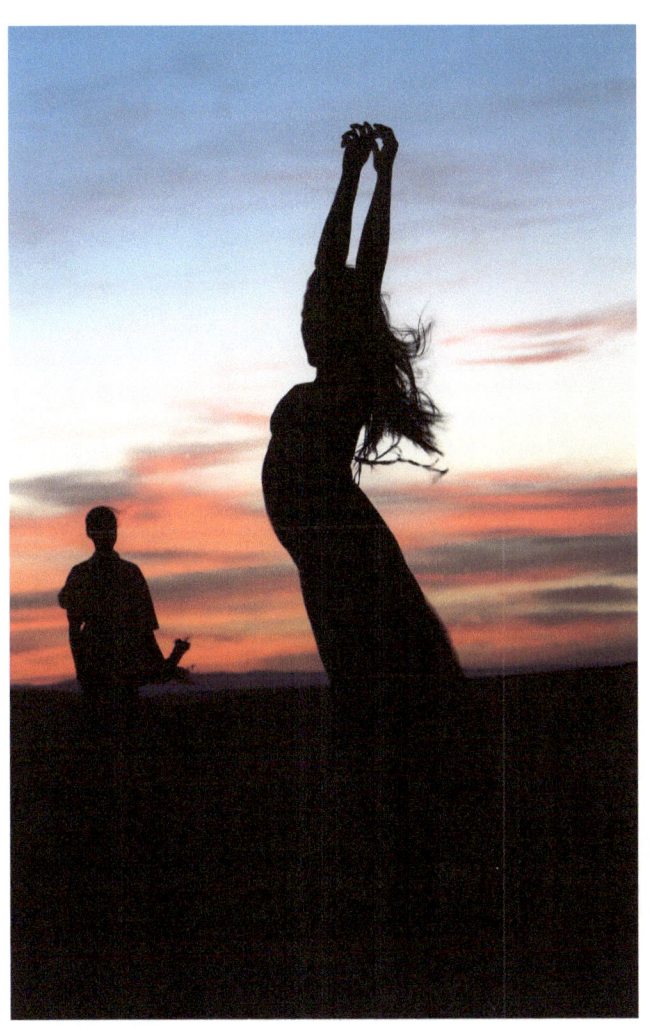

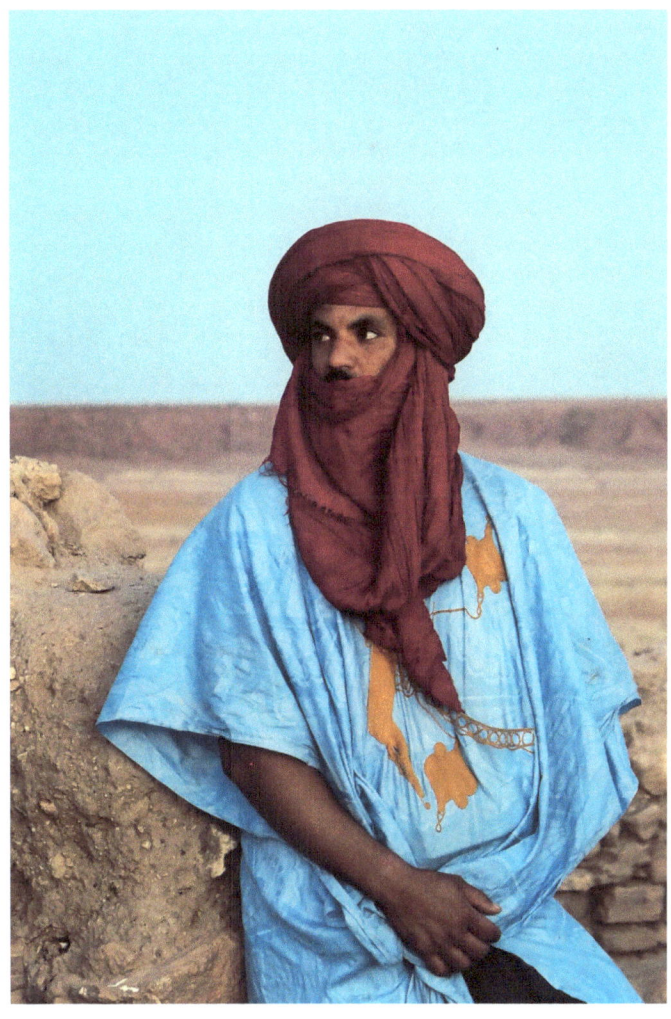

39

39

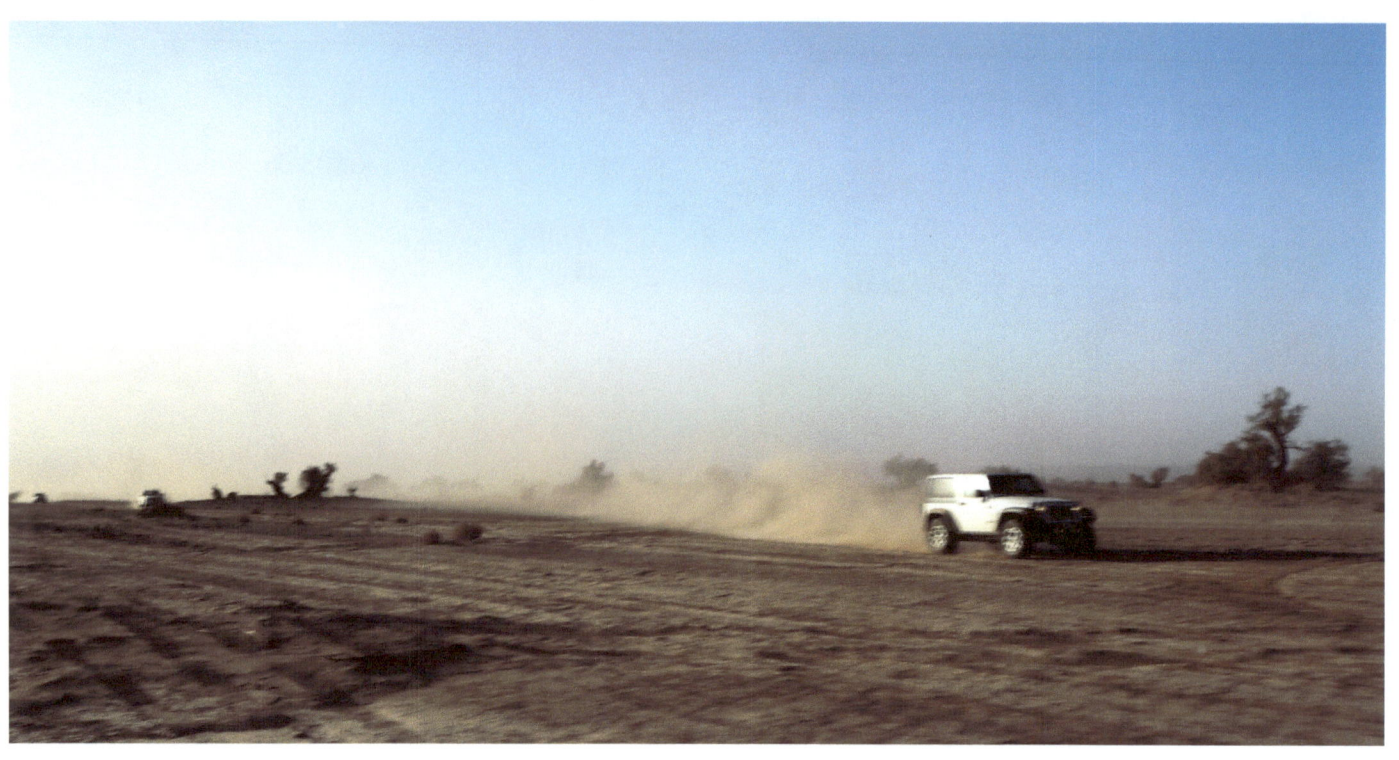

To move forward into the great Sahara we rely on desert nomads who take us to their camp with powerful SUVs in an adventurous desert run.

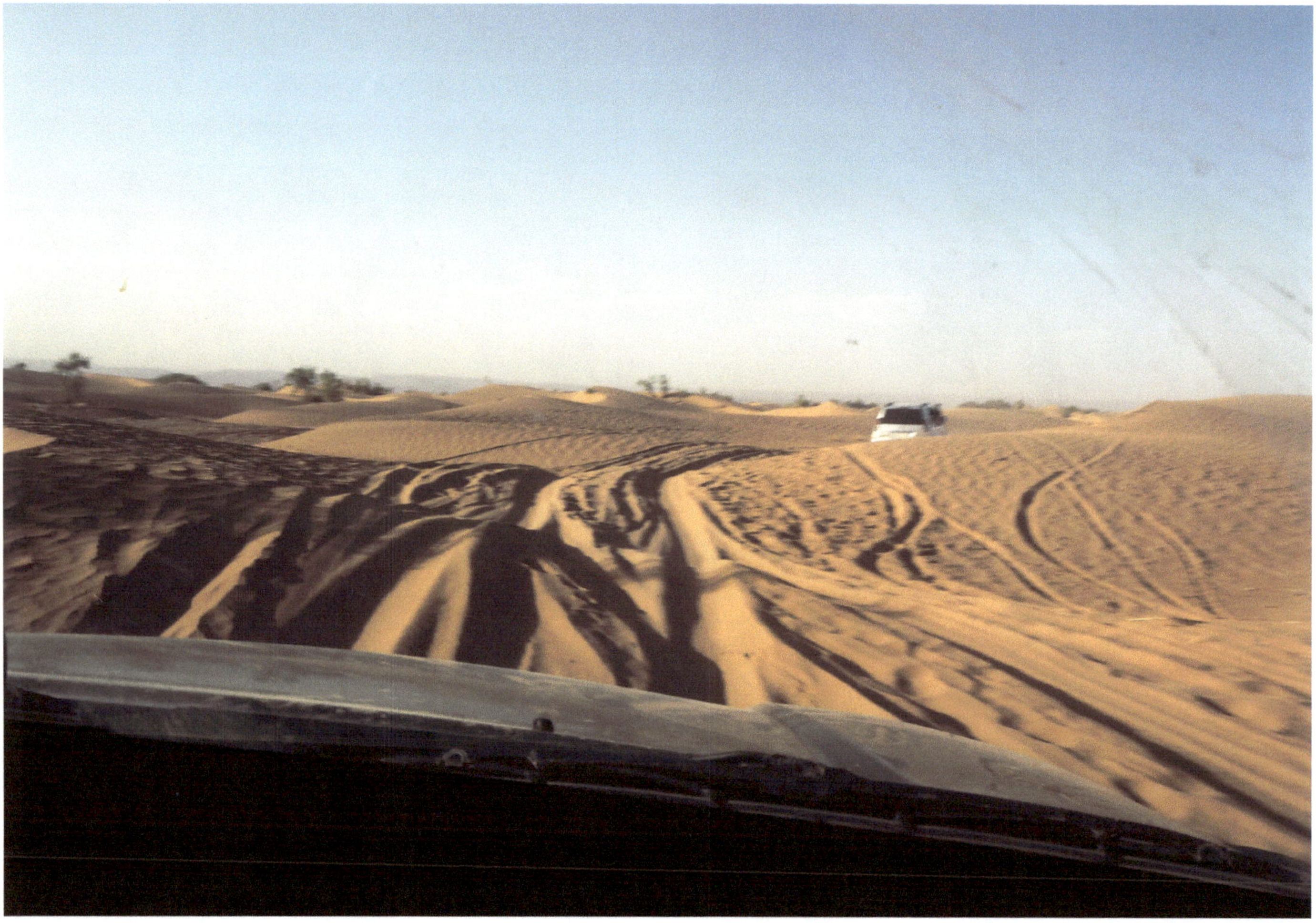

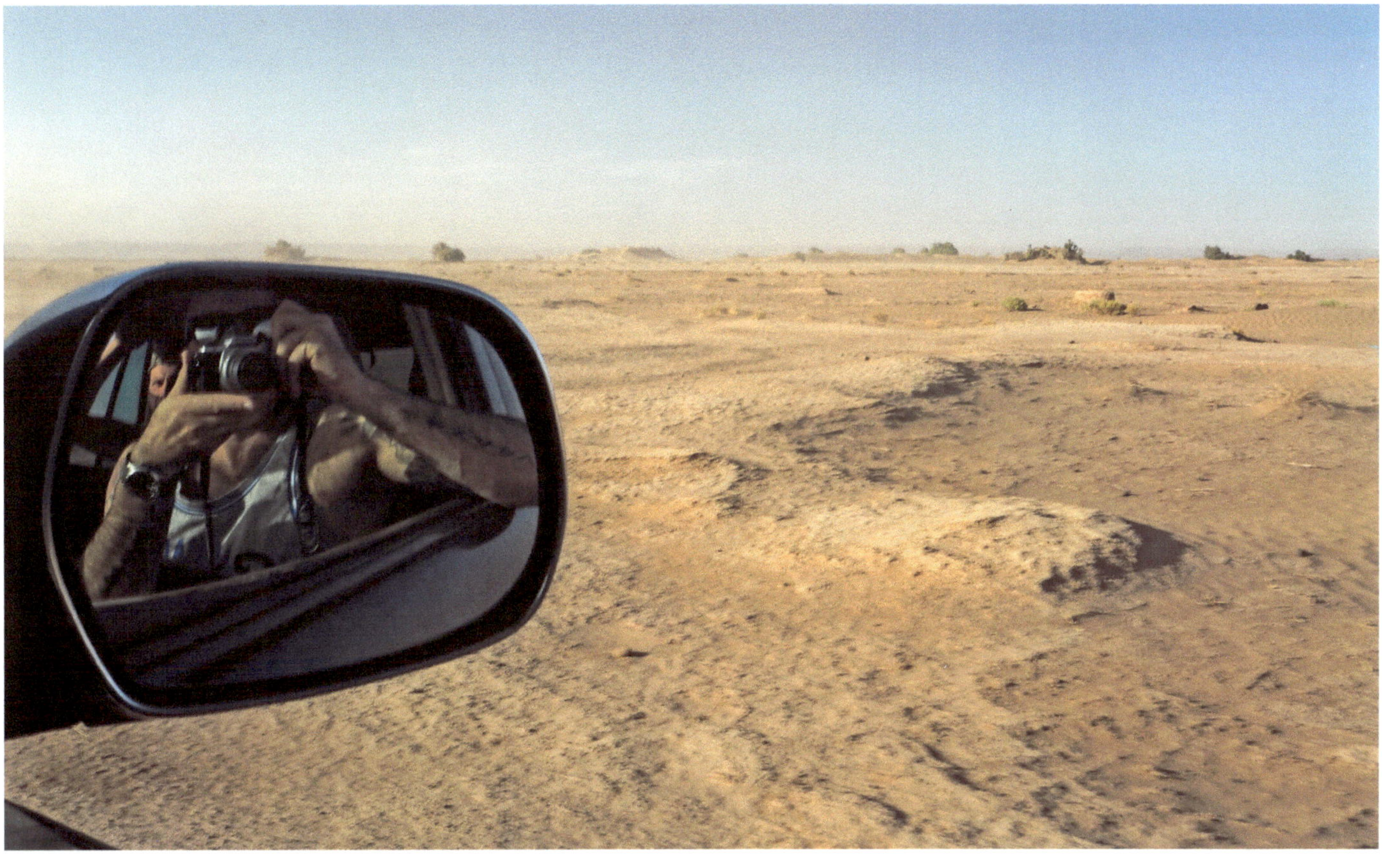

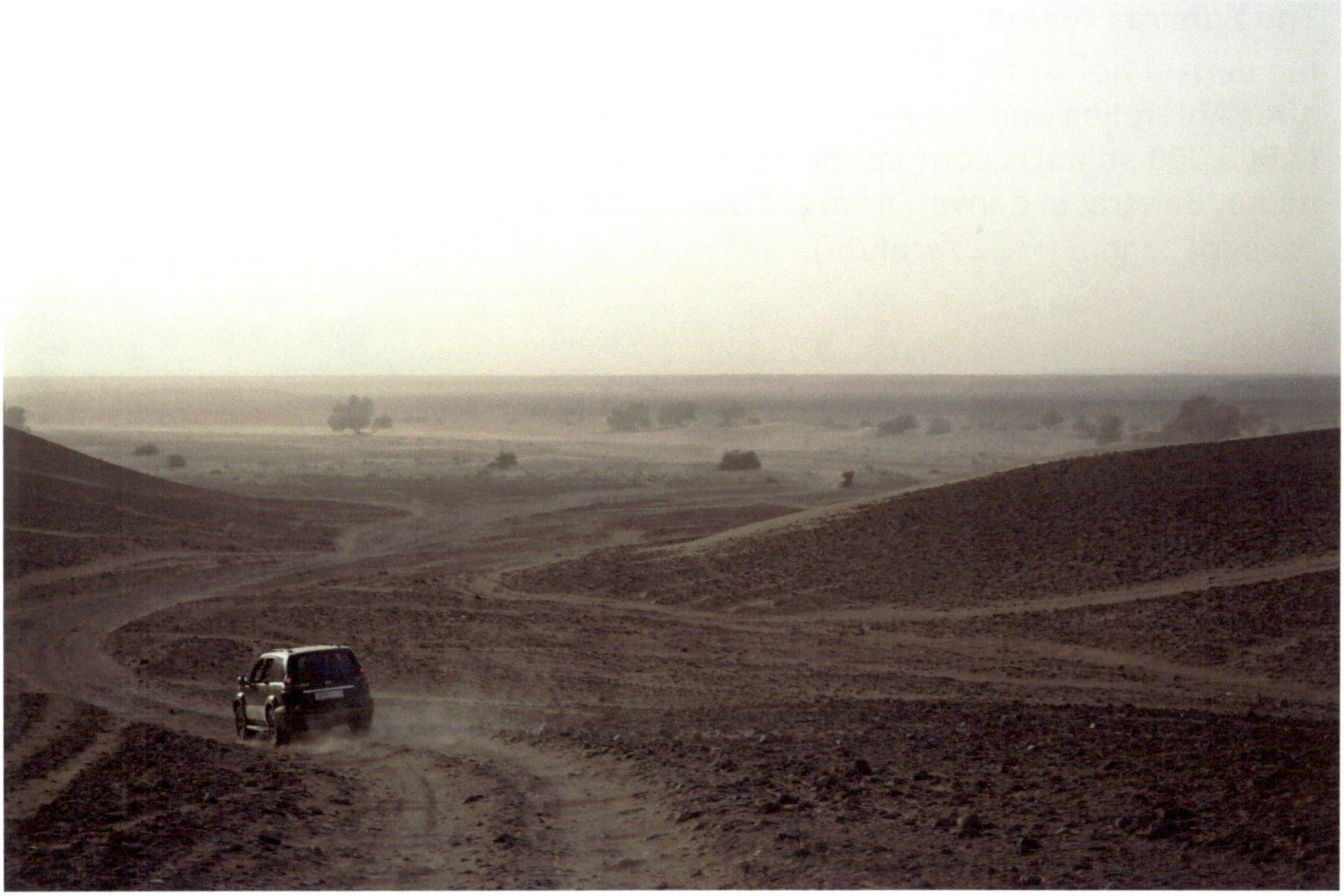

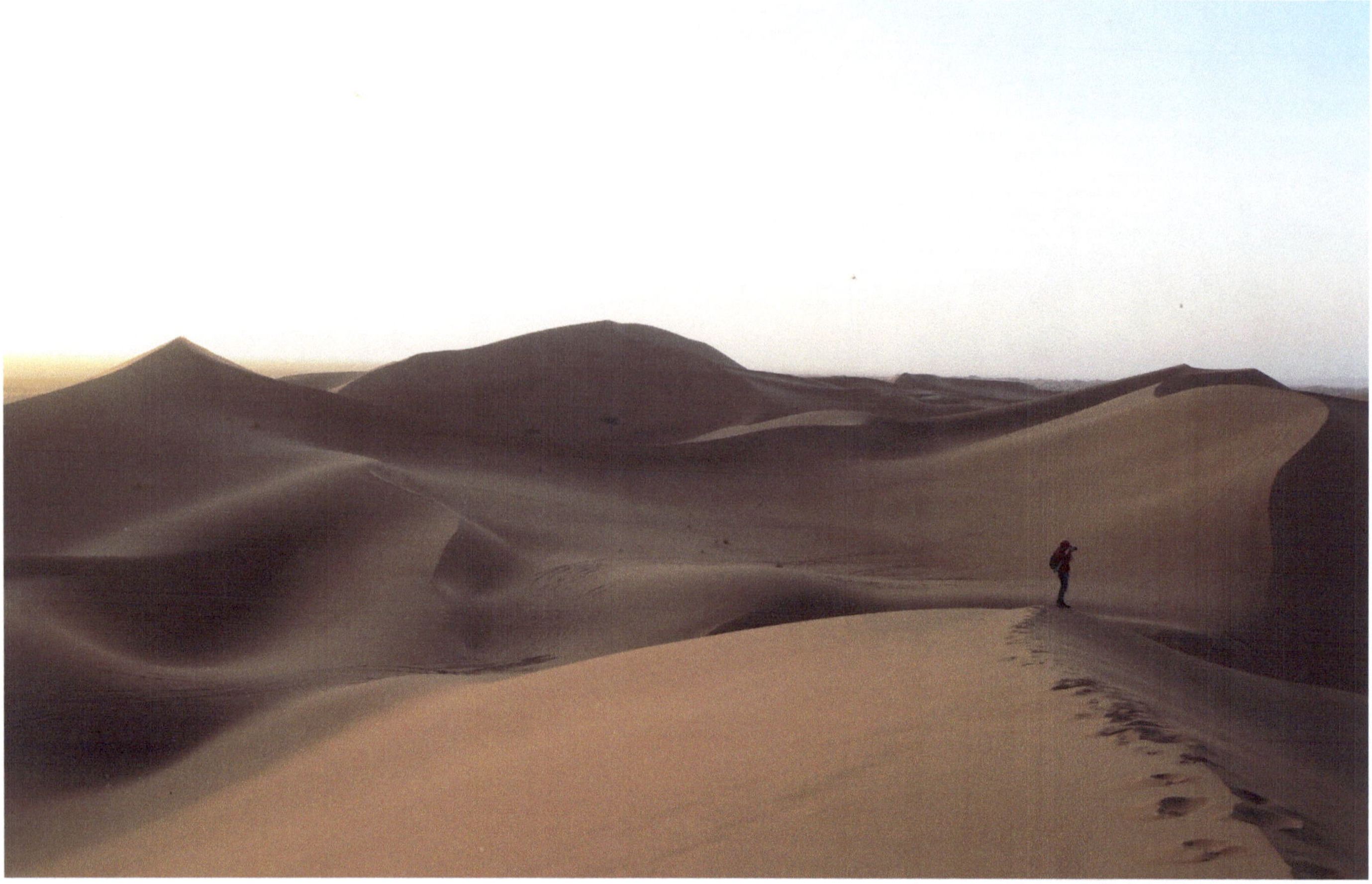

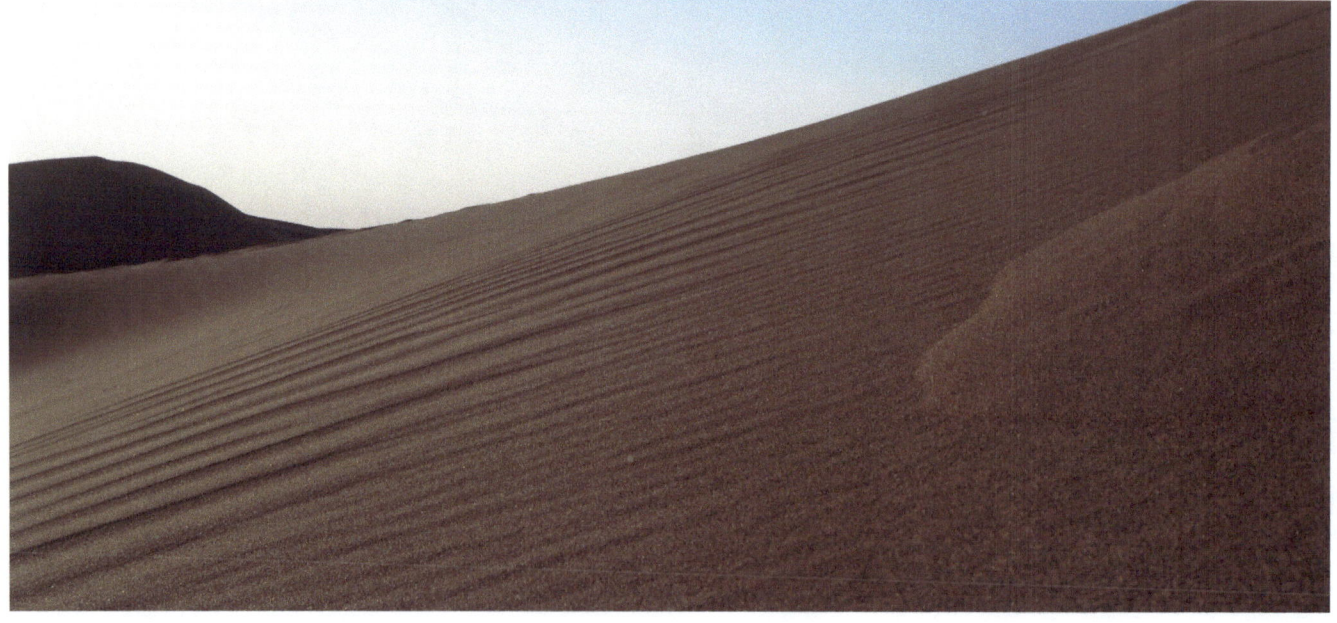

The **Sahara** (Arabic: الصحراء الكبرى, aṣ-ṣaḥrā' al-kubrá, 'the Great Desert') is the largest hot desert in the world, and the third largest desert overall after Antarctica and the Arctic. Its area of 9,200,000 square kilometres (3,600,000 sq mi) is comparable to the area of China or the United States. The name 'Sahara' is derived from a dialectal Arabic word for "desert", ṣaḥra (صحرا /'sˤaħra/).

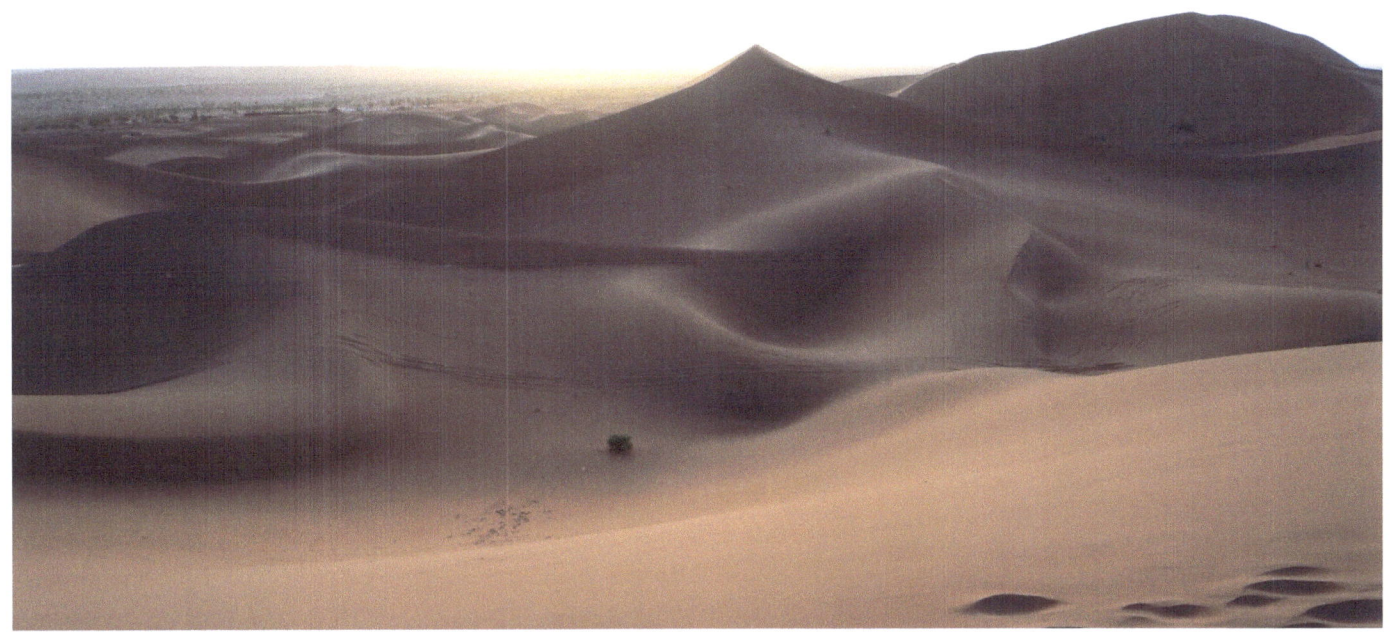

The immensity of the sahara, with its shapes, its curves, its infinite horizon, makes a man feel like a grain of sand, microscopic yet part of the whole.

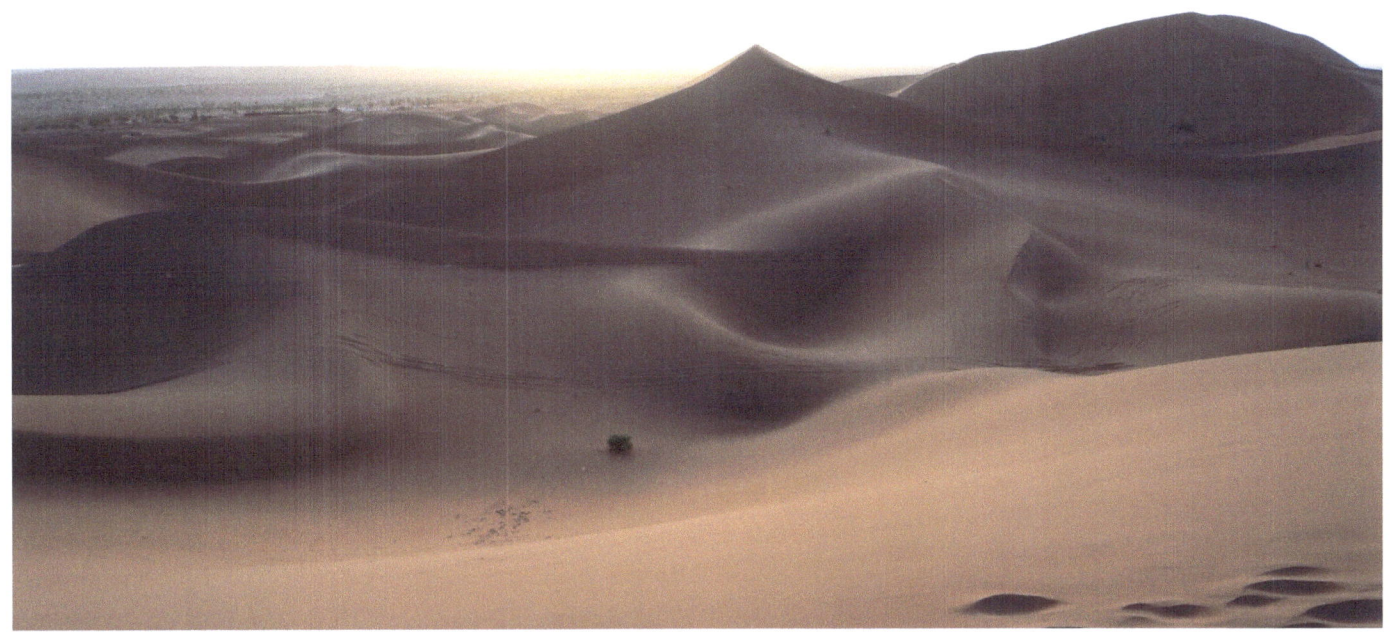

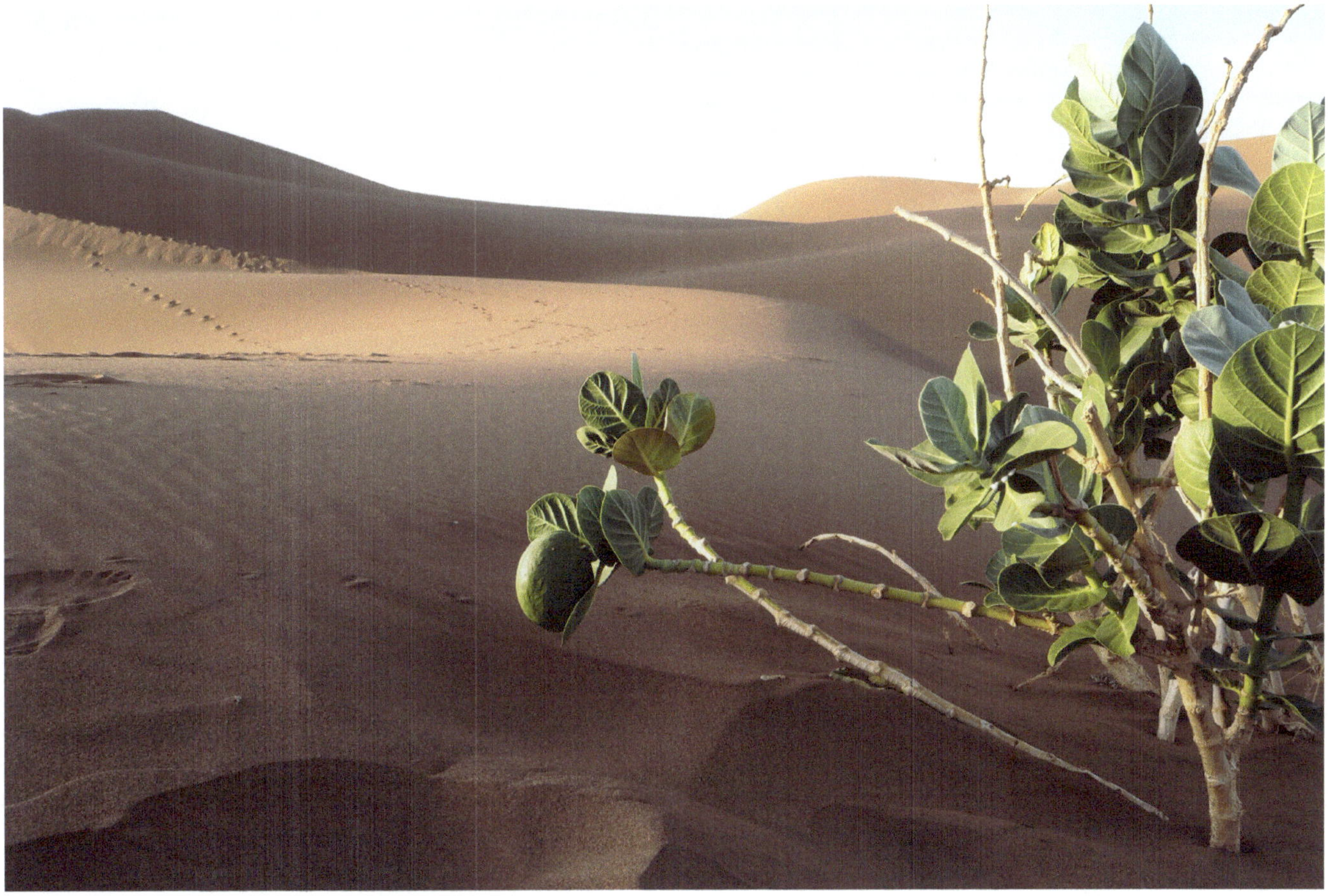

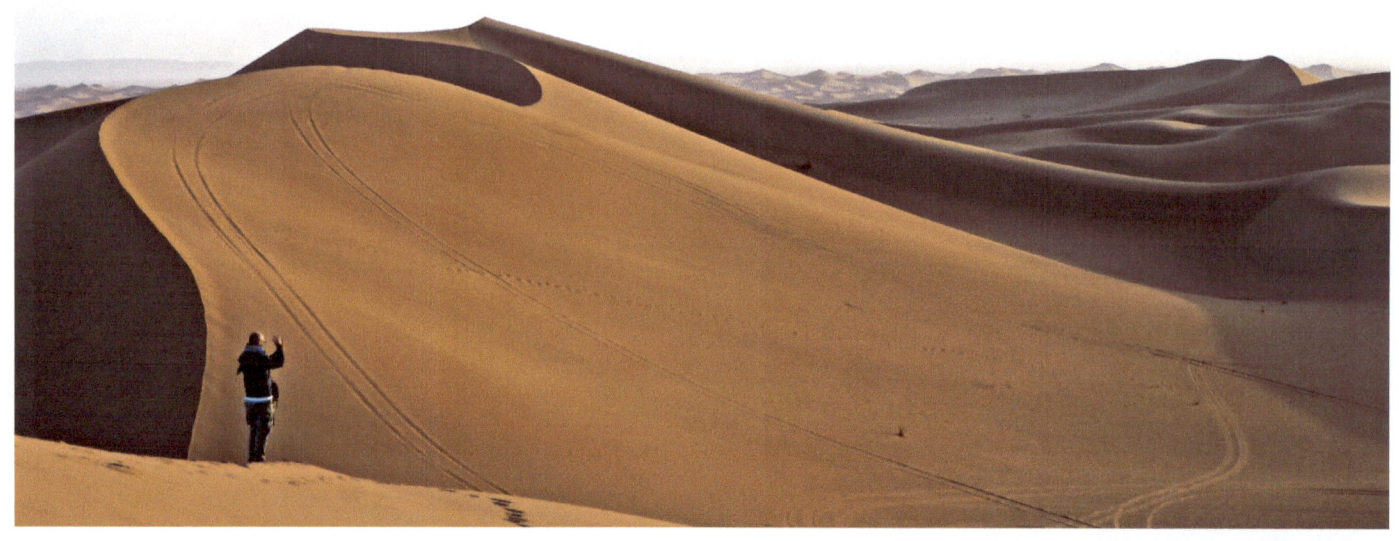

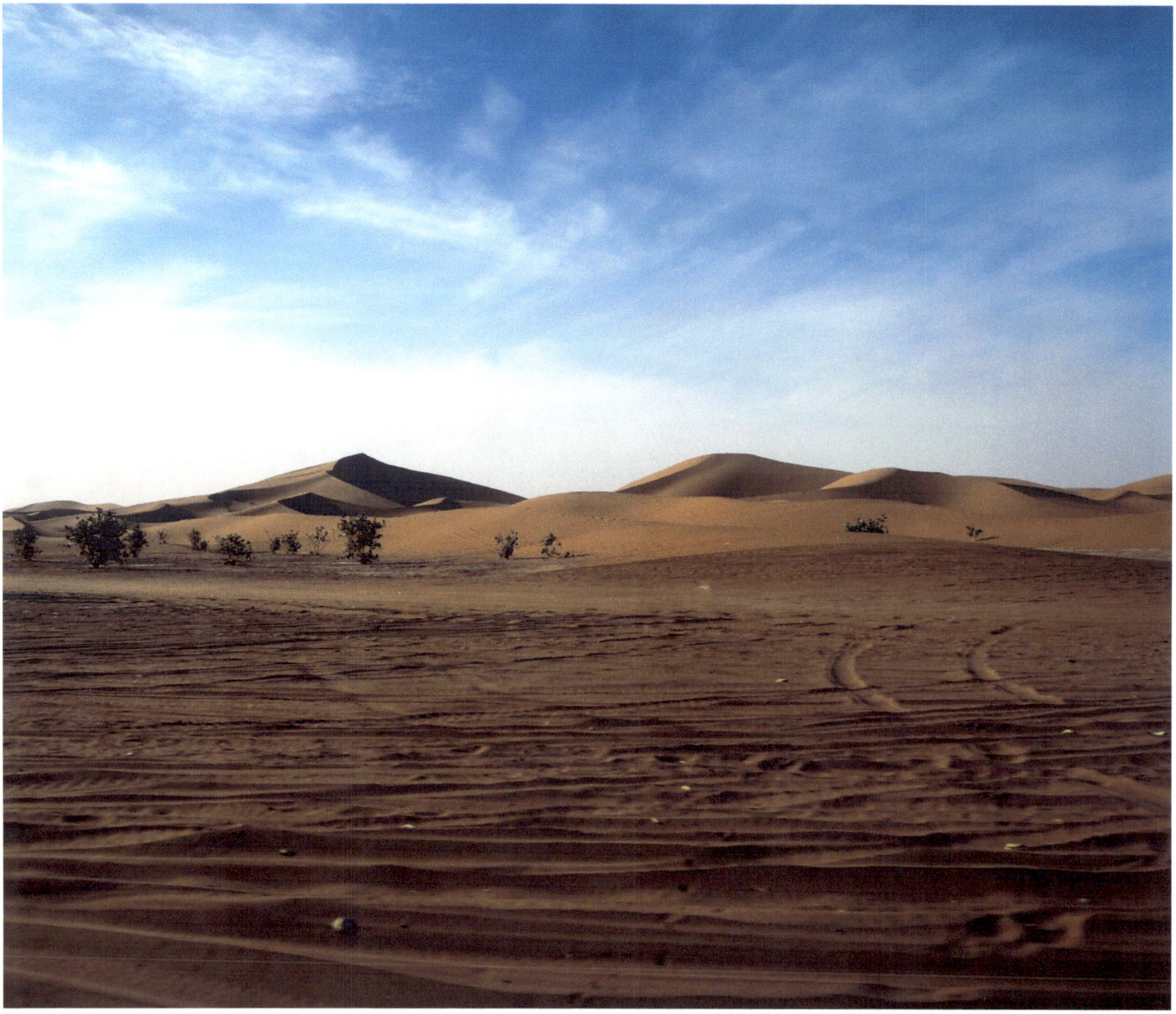

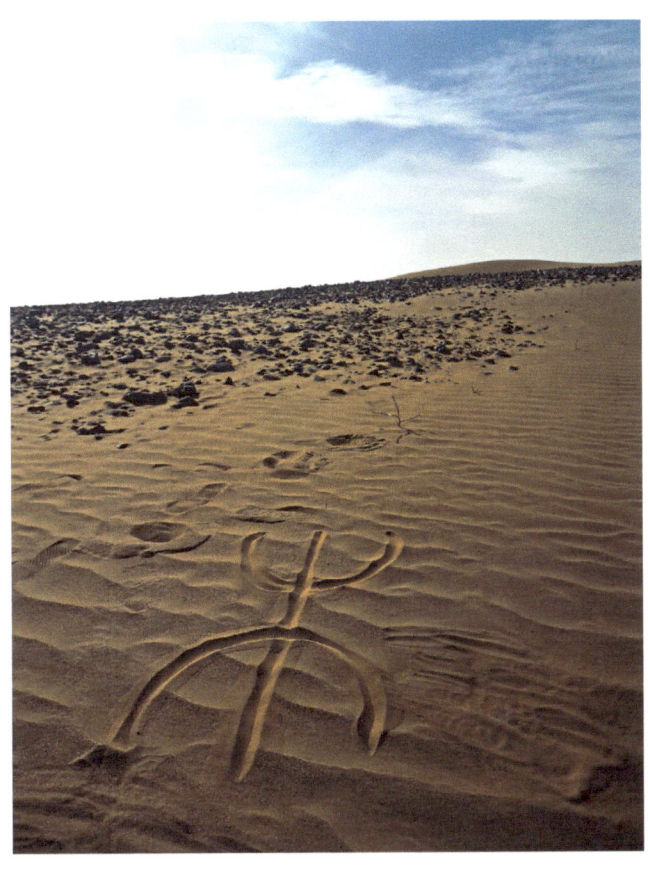

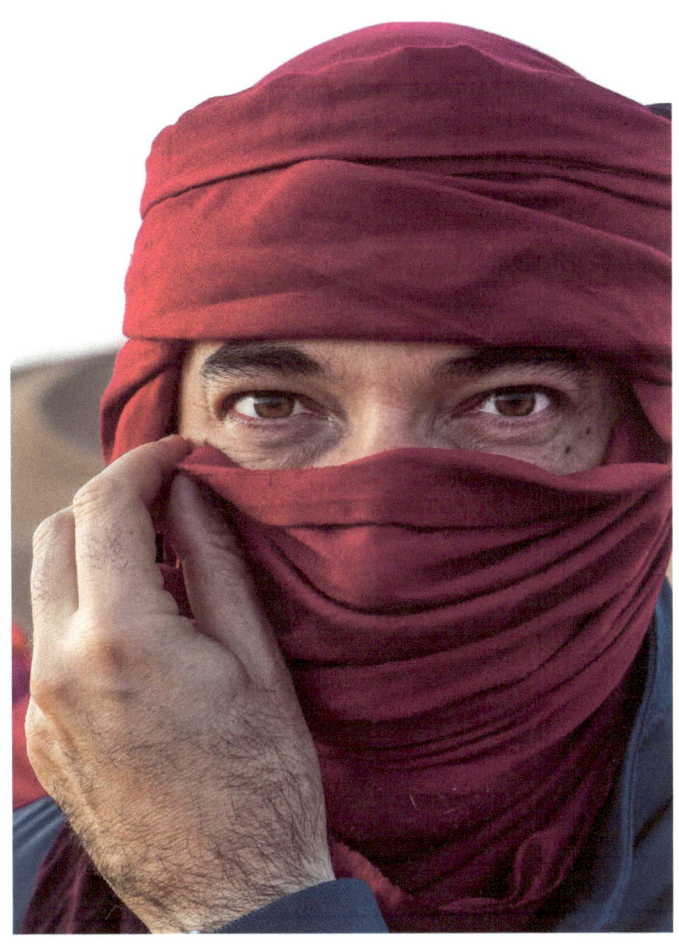

The symbol of the "Amazigh", the free men of the desert

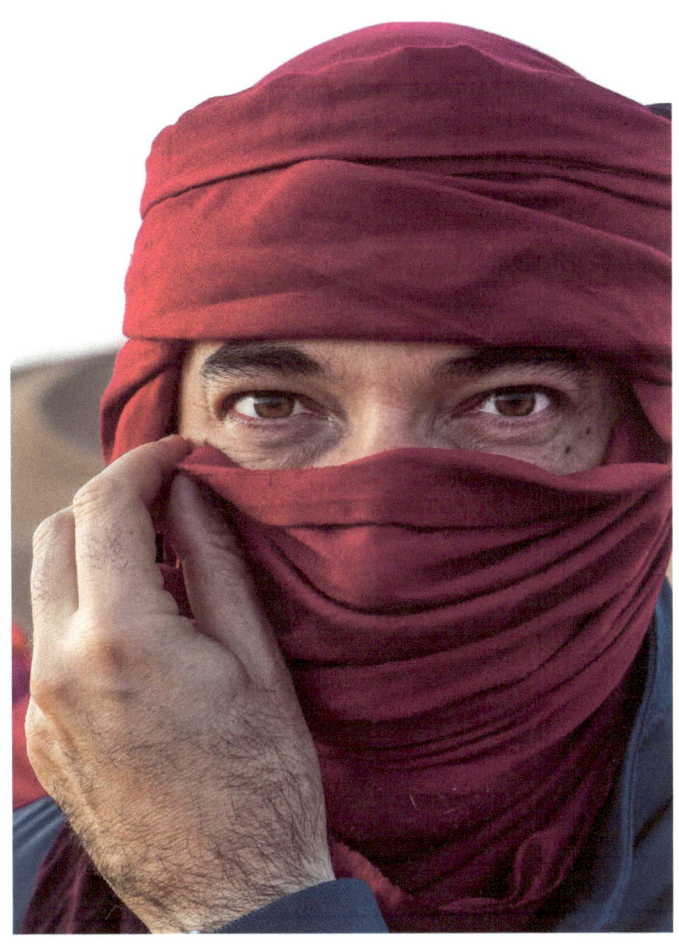

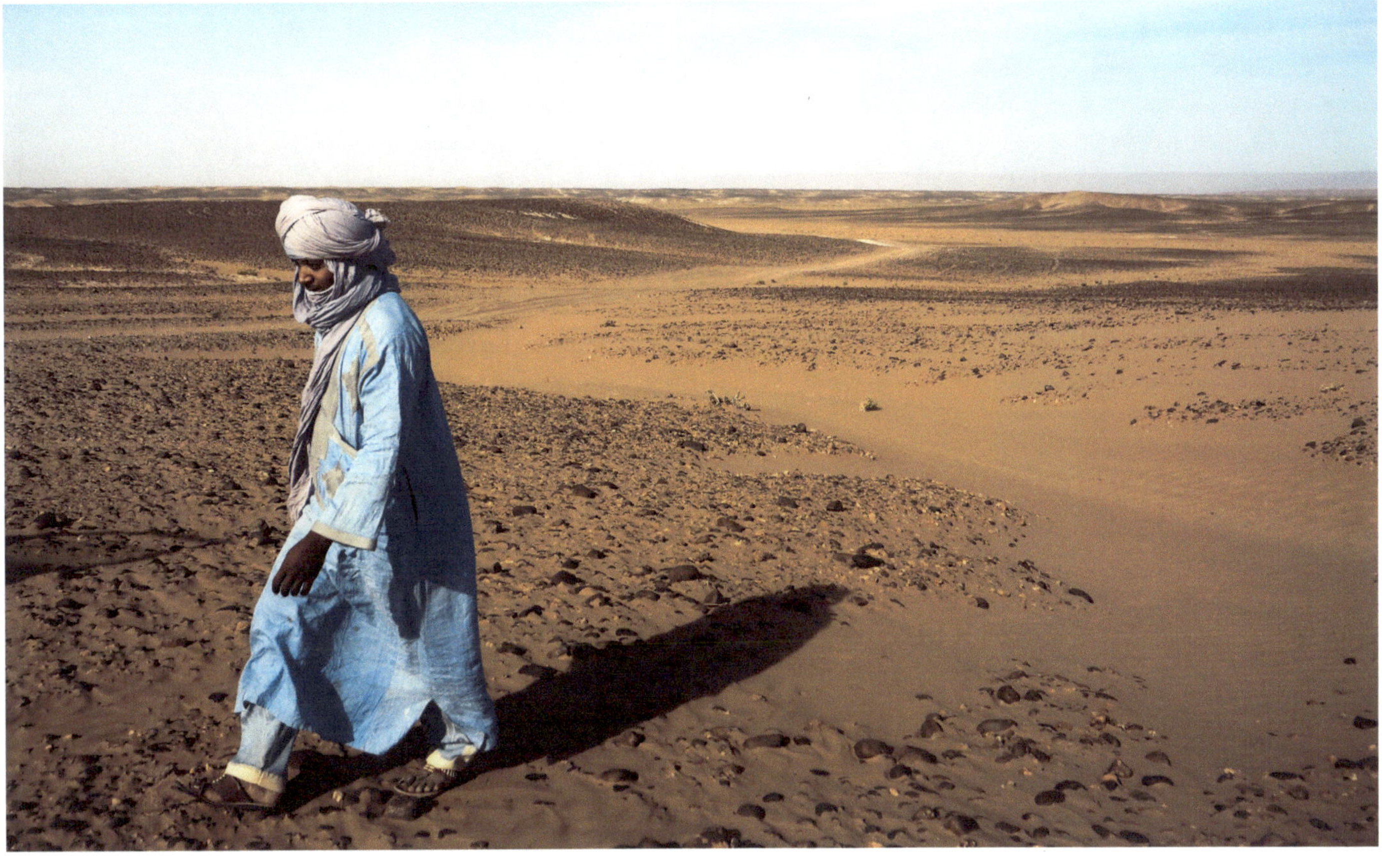

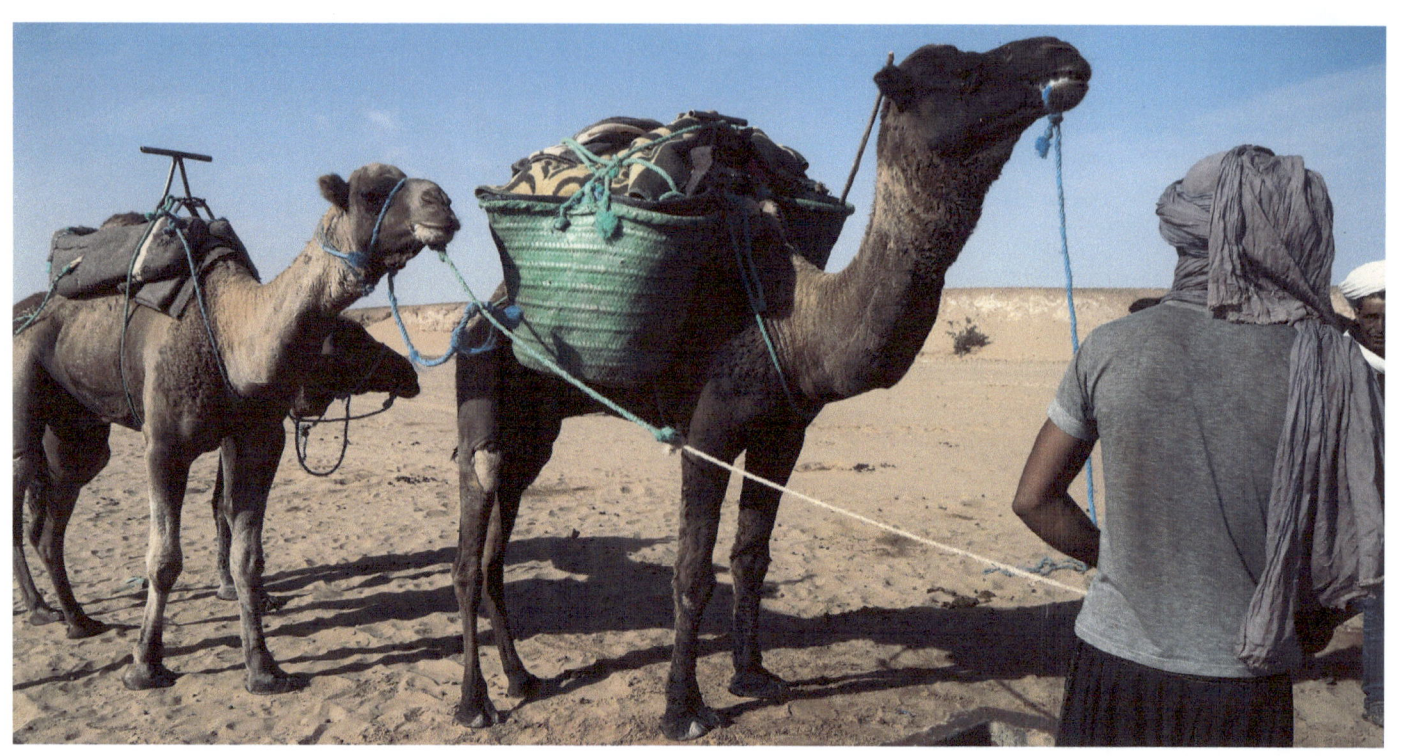

on the way back we meet a Nomad caravan intent on getting the camels to quench their thirst at a well, and we decide to give them a hand

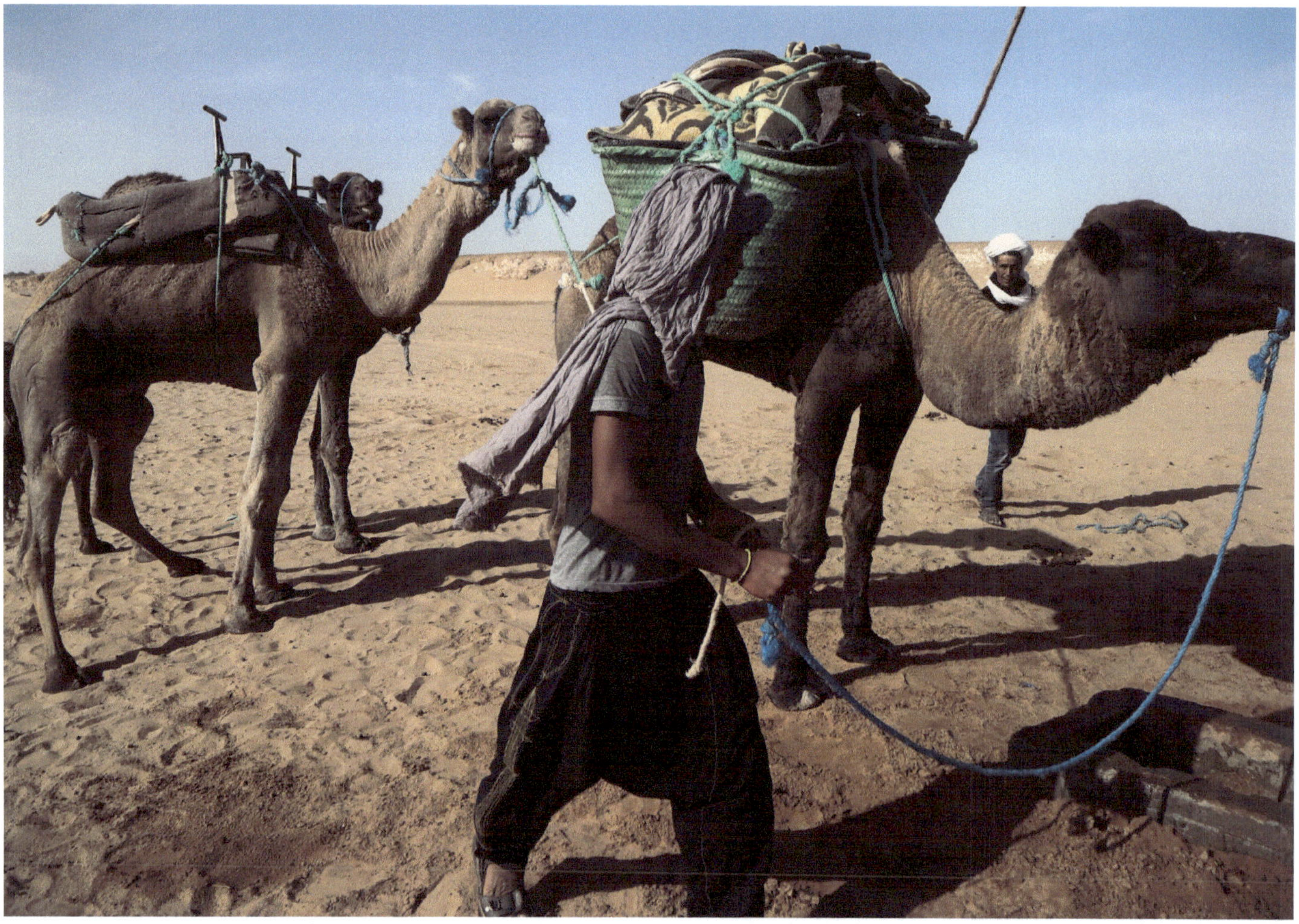

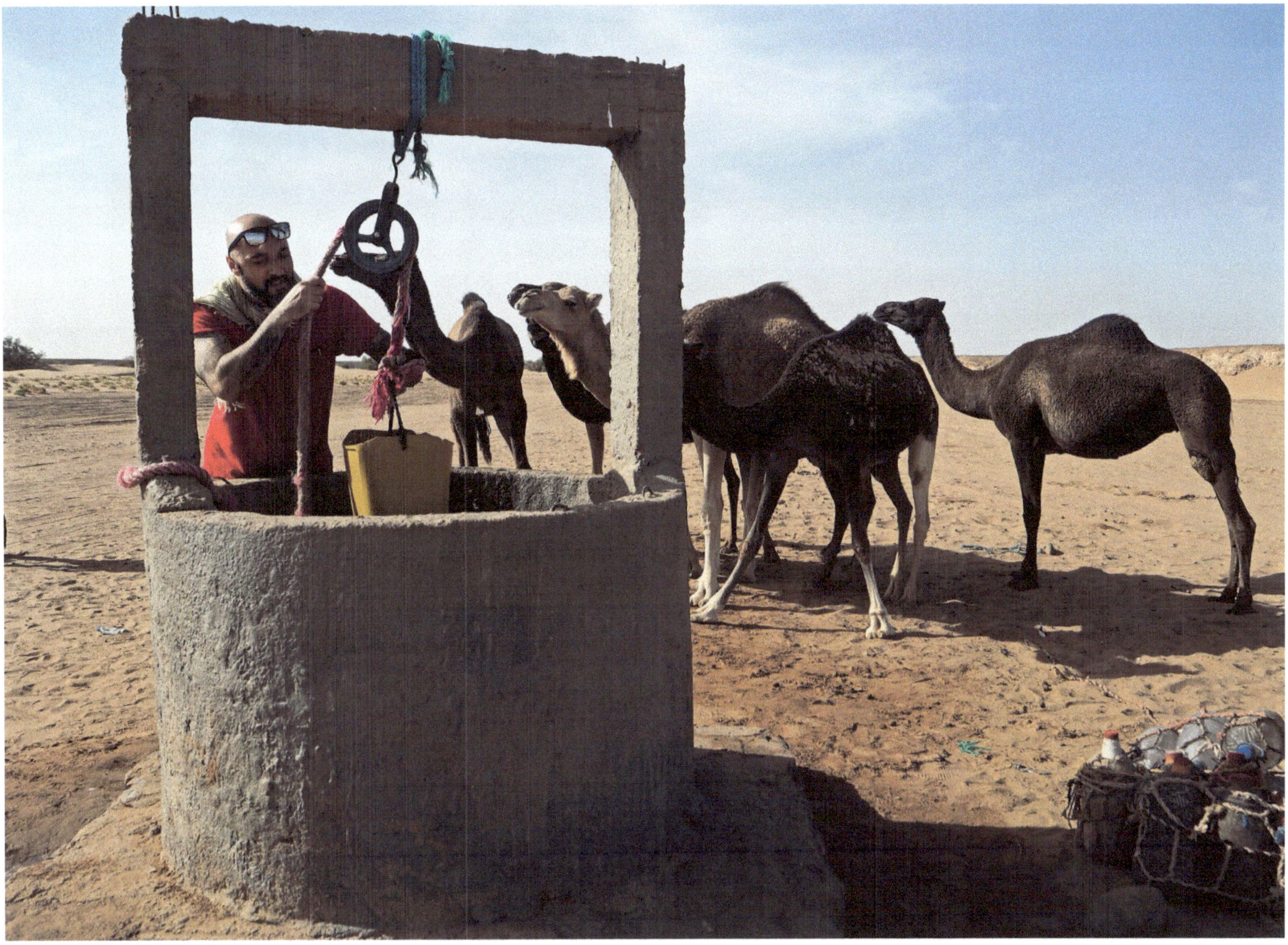

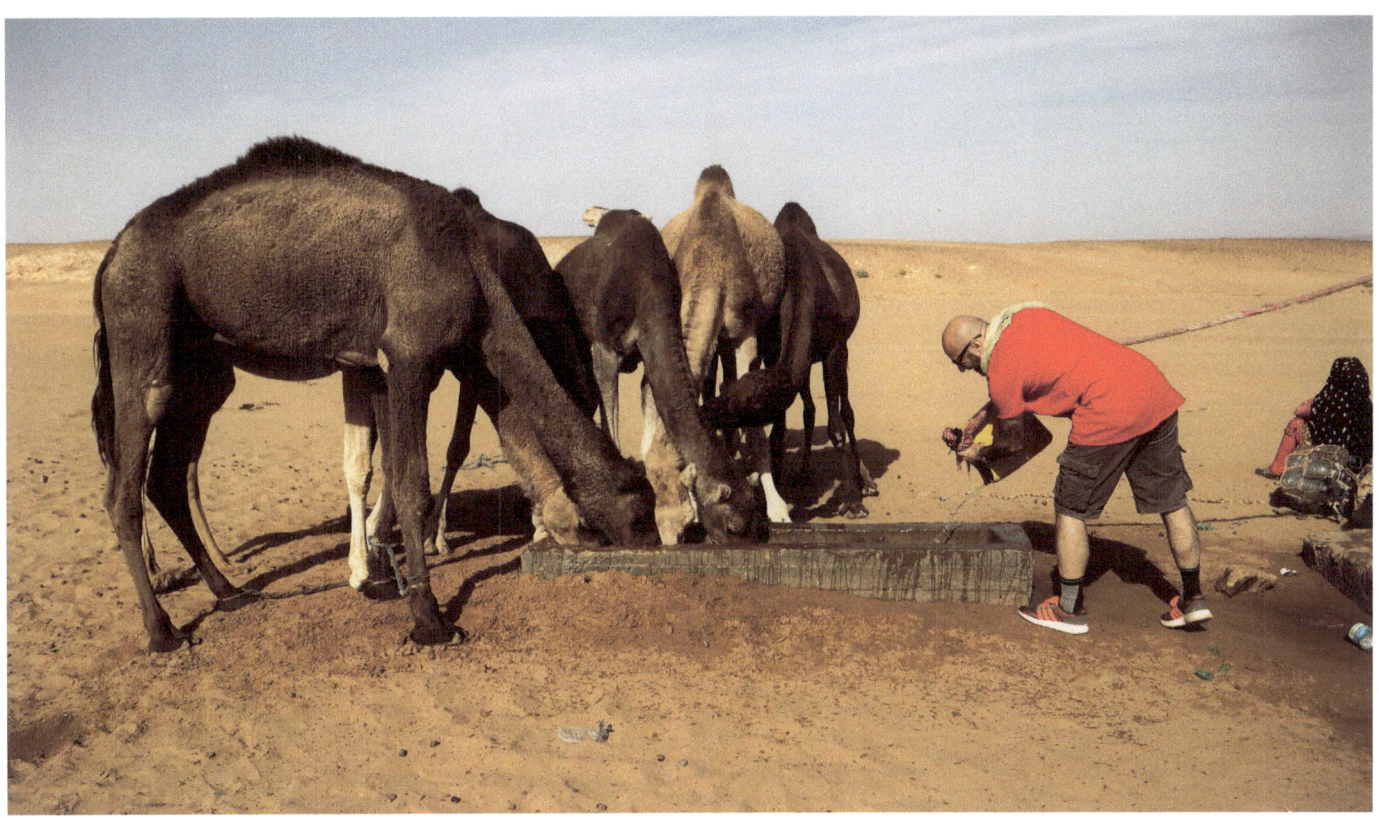

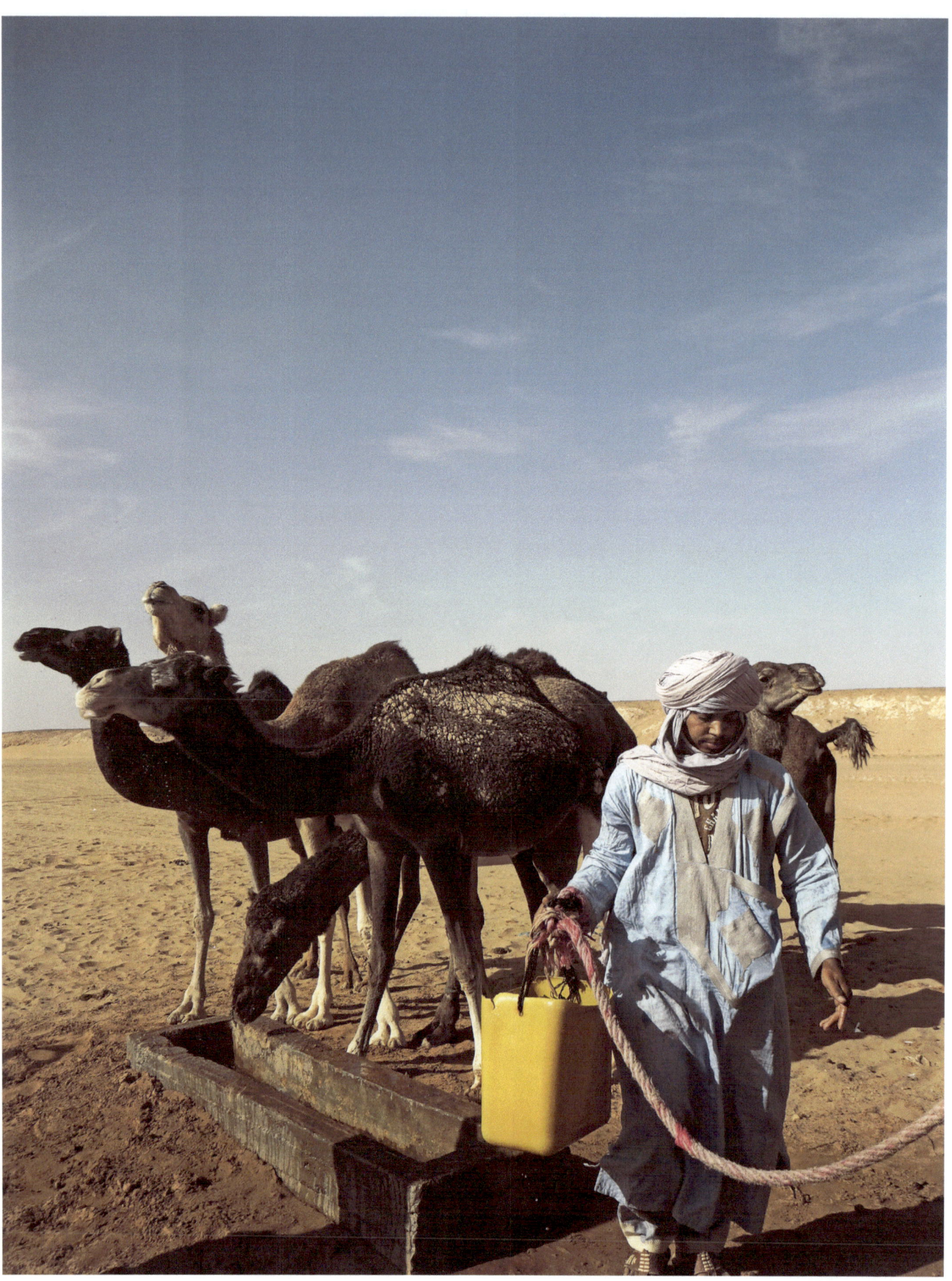

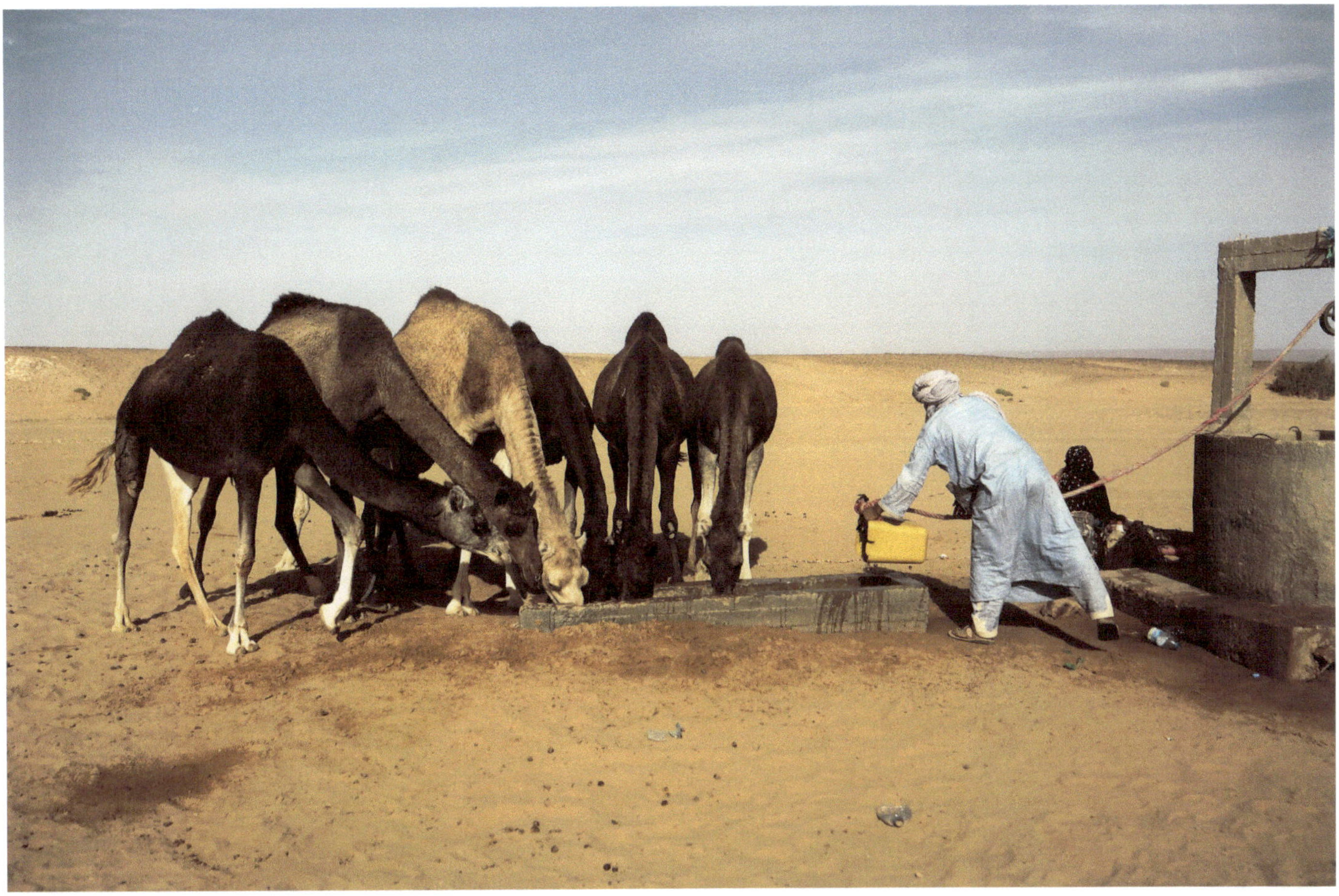

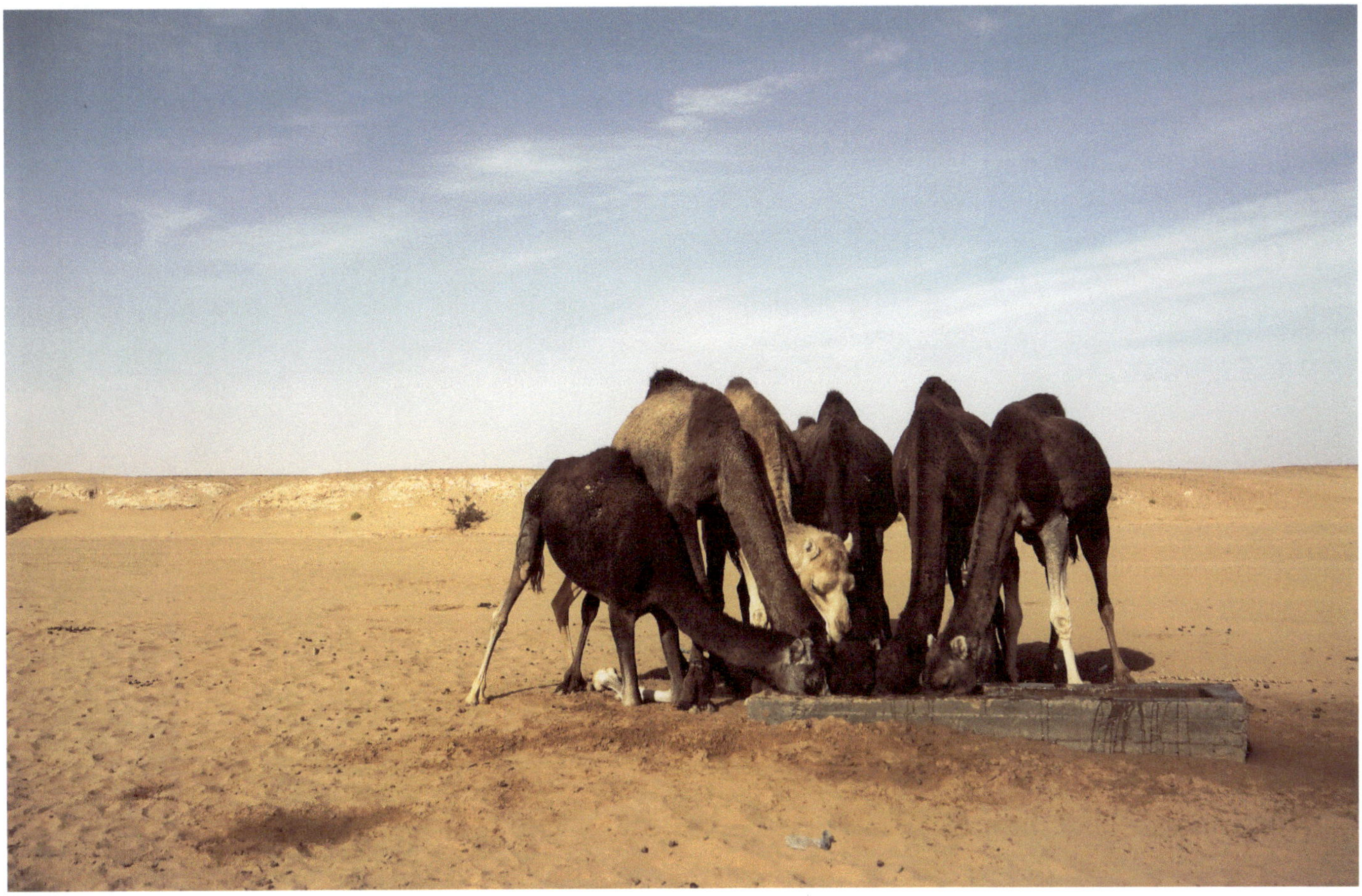

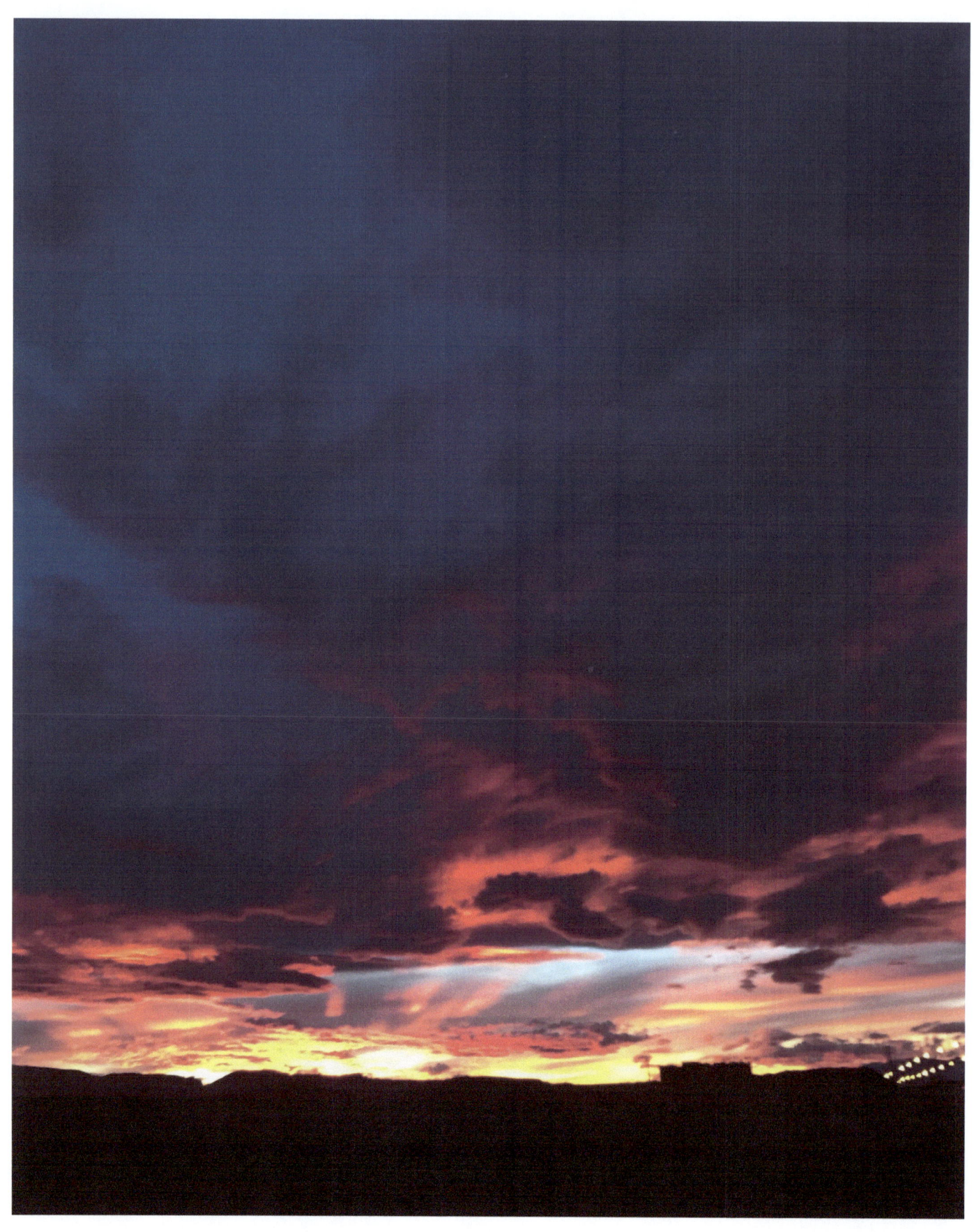

Morocco gifts us with one last incredible sunset before saying goodbye

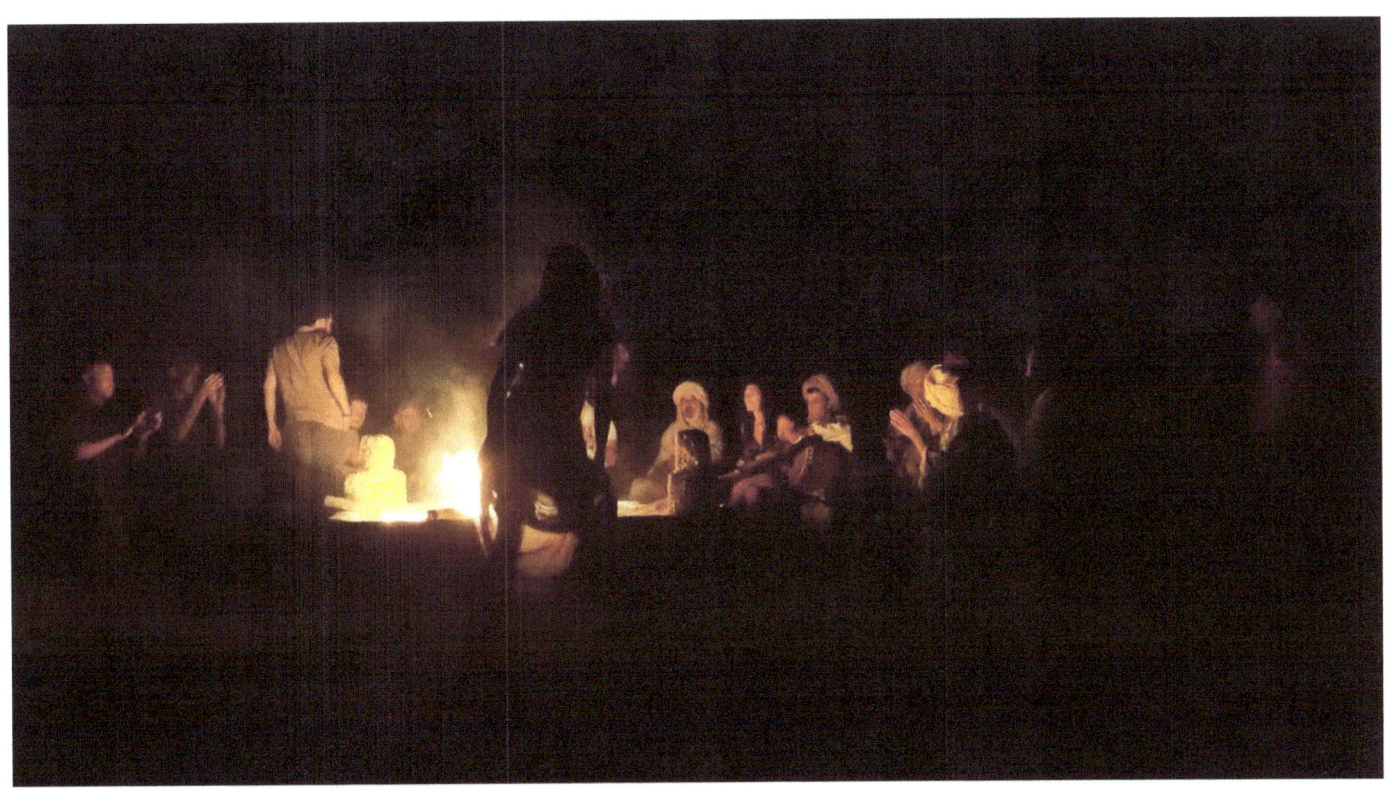

"The fire is the cinema of the desert, the sky is the cinema of the Kings" -
(Berber saying)

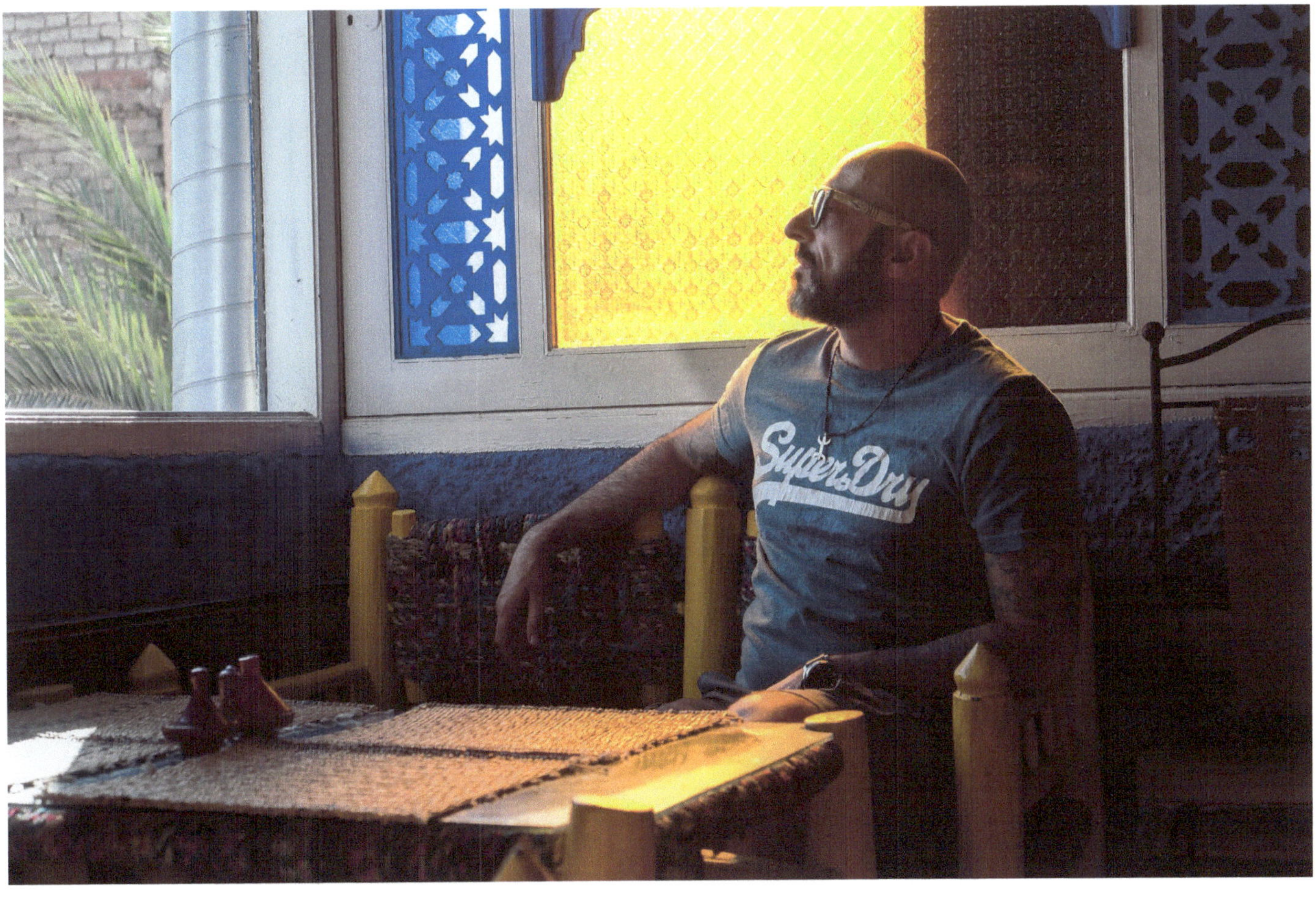